LOOKING BACK AT MONKGATE & THE GROVES YORK

by

Avril E. Webster Appleton

© Avril E. Webster Appleton 2002

Reprint 2009

ISBN 978 0 9543463 0 0

Published by

Reeder Publications
18 Whitby Drive, York, England, YO31 1EX
Telephone 01904 424872

Printed by

York Publishing Services
64 Hallfield Road, Layerthorpe, York YO31 7ZQ
www.yps-publishing.co.uk

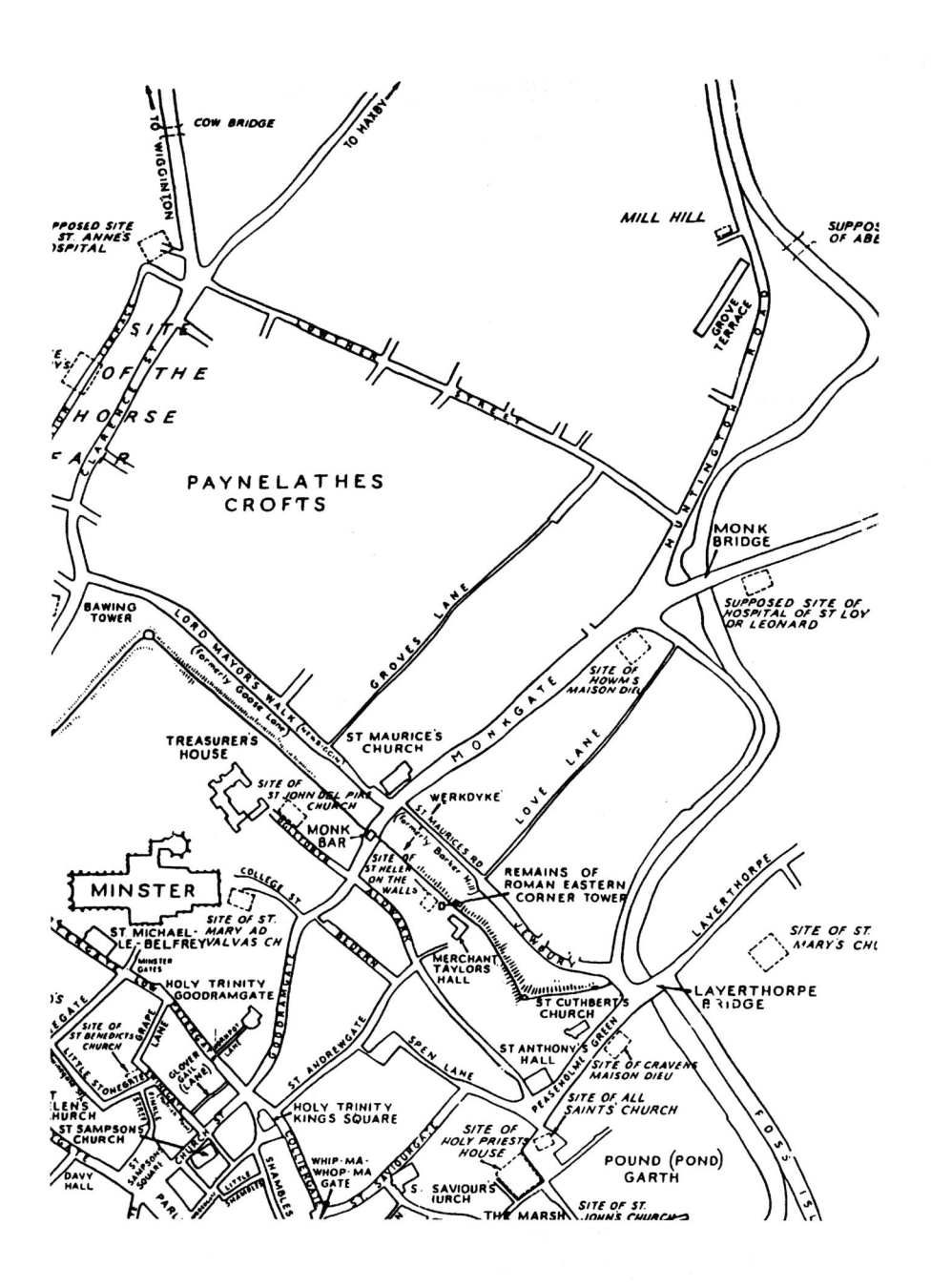

Medieval Map – Paynelath's Crofts

CONTENTS

FOREWORD vii

INTRODUCTION AND ACKNOWLEDGEMENTS viii

Chapter I Early Times

Monkgate 1
Monk Bar 3
Paynelath's Crofts 3
Newbiggin 5
Old St. Maurice's Church 5
Lord Mayor's Walk 6
St. Maurice's Road 6
Jewbury 8
Haxby Road 9
The Horse Fair 9
St Mary's Hospital 10
Monk Bridge 10
Maison Dieu of Robert Holme 10

Chapter II Life in Georgian and Victorian Times

Church Warden's Accounts 13
Pew Rents 14
Bowman Family 14
William Scawin 15
Grove House 18
Eliza Tabor 18
The Hirstwood Family 19
The New Workhouse 19
Anne Harrison's Hospital 20
Thomas Agar's Hospital 21
The County Hospital 21

Chapter III Housing Development

Early Houses 24
Monkgate Houses 24
George Hudson 24
William Fawdington 26
William Hayes 27
74 Monkgate 28
More Monkgate Houses 28

Lime Tree House School	29
North West Side	30
Cuckow Nest	30
Bearpark Family	31
Speculative Building	32
Bowling Green Lane	34

Chapter IV Early Schools

Manchester College	36
Archbishop Holgate's Grammar School	36
St. John's Training College	37
St. John's Secondary Modern School	39
St. John's Training College for Women	39
Grey Coat School	39
Miss Bazzard	42
Memories of Grey Coat Girls	42
The Webster Family	42
St Thomas' Church School	43
Brook Street School	45
St. Wilfrid's School	46
Park Grove School	48

Chapter V To Church or Chapel

St. Thomas' Church	52
Church Minutes	52
Guides and Brownies	56
St. Maurice's Church	56
Groves Methodist Chapel	59
Brook Street Chapel	59
The New Chapel	59
Monkgate Methodist Chapel	61
Archie Sargent	62
Memories of Choir Members	63

Chapter VI Life in the 1920's and 1930's

Mrs Webster's Memories	65
Memories of Park Grove School	66
Mrs Morton's Memories	68
The Fowler Family	70
The Lovely Family	71
Mr Thompson's Memories	73
Alderman Hutchinson's Memories	73
St. Hilda's Home	74

    Wilfrid Cousin's Memories 76
    Margaret Dyson's Memories.. 76
    Nellie Mooring's Memories... 77
    Brian Sargent's Memories.. 80
    Groves Working Men's' Club 80
    Clarence Street.. 81
    Clarence Working Men's Club 81

Chapter VII War Years

    Preparing For War 85
    Rationing and Ration Books.. 85
    Air Raids 86
    Damage 87
    Memories of Air Raids 87
    Holidays at Home 88
    V.E. Celebrations.. 89

Chapter VIII Memories of the 1940's and 1950's

    Mr Lake's Memories 93
    Mrs Ros's Memories... 94
    Mr Myers's Memories 96
    Mr and Mrs Marshall's Memories 98
    Mr Martindale's Memories 99
    Mr Elsegoood's Memories... 100
    Mr Hardcastle's Memories 102
    Mr Fairclough's Memories 103
    Mr Woodcock's Memories 104
    Mr Pickard's Memories... 105
    Mrs Cole's Memories 106
    Demolition and After 109

Front Cover: Monkgate c1840 (Courtesy Mr M Powell)
Inside Front & Back Cover: OS MAP 1930 (Crown Copyright)

FOREWORD

The history of York is carried through with a history of Monkgate and the Groves, a fortunate location close to the city. As a resident through the war years and beyond I have many memories, happy and sad, but I'm mostly comforted by my recollections of the many times of pleasure and excitement as a child.

The character of the area was in the location and the lifestyle of its locals. From the poor and disadvantaged to the middle-class and professional residents, everyone found their place in the unique life they all enjoyed.

Every where was convenient and a few paces, or a short walk away. All food and drink vendors, traders and merchants were on first name terms with their clients. Every street had a selection of residents with remedies for every ailment, from birthing babies through childhood diseases to "laying out the deceased".

The near city location gave all the advantages of commerce, retail and industry through its residents ranging from chocolate and sweet production to railway carriage manufacture with many other light industrial concerns.

Best of all were sounds and sights, Minster bell at noon on a cloudy day, the smell of chocolate, caramel or peppermint. The green areas of the Moat along the Bar Walls, the newly-mown grass of the "Wiggy Road" fields, Monk Stray, the peace and tranquillity of the River Foss.

The Monkgate and Groves residents went to all the modern wars and many died. Many suffered too but their spirit and memories would sustain them for all of their lives.

Geoff Lake
(Ex-Groves resident, now living in Australia)

INTRODUCTION

The idea of a book on the Groves and Monkgate came to me as I was recently walking through this area en route to the District Hospital. The last time I had spent much time here was in the 1940's and 50's when I stayed with a friend who lived in Garden Street. But where was Garden Street now? Where was Jackson Street, Backhouse, Bedford and Princess Street? Where were all those familiar shops I had known so well from those days, Benson's bike shop, Atkinson's hardware shop, the Co-op and all the fish and chip shops. The area had changed dramatically and in their places I found large blocks of flats and maisonettes.

The periphery of this area had changed too. St. Maurice's Church with its familiar clock I relied on to get me home on time from the dances in the church hall in St. Maurice's Road, gone! The old County Hospital with its long corridors and wards with open verandas, now housed luxury flats.

Talking to people who remembered this area before these changes and listening to the stories of some of the many shopkeepers and characters that had abounded here I thought it was important to record it all before it was lost for ever. I set myself the task of not only recalling those days but tracing the history of the area from early times to the 1960's when many of the houses were demolished.

Because of space and economy I do not claim this book to be a concise history of the area and I apologise to anyone who thinks that their family should have been mentioned. I shall leave it to others to record in more detail specific buildings and topics I have only touched on. How ever I hope that this book brings back many happy memories to past residents and to present and future ones, gives them a fascinating glimpse of life in the 'Old Groves and Monkgate'.

Avril E. Webster Appleton. June. 2002

ACKNOWLEDGEMENTS

My thanks go to all who have helped me with this book. To my son David for all his hard work helping me compile my work into a book form. To my husband Cliff and all my family for all their encouragement and understanding. To Rita and staff at York City Archives, the Borthwick Institute, and staff at York Reference and Tang Hall libraries. To The Oliver Sheldon Trust for help with the cost of publication and to John Bullivant and staff for all their help and advice. To David Poole and Mike Race for help and information. A special thanks to Mike and Jan Powell for information, encouragement and help with the photographs. Grateful thanks also to all those past and present residents of Monkgate and the Groves who have loaned photographs and given valuable information and to every one who has made this publication possible.

Avril E. Webster Appleton

CHAPTER I
EARLY TIMES

Monkgate

In his great work on York, Eboracum, written in 1746, Francis Drake described Monkgate, as "a fair broad street well paved and pretty well built up". He recalled that there had been a leper hospital, dedicated to St. Loy, at Monk Bridge, but he did not know how Monkgate, meaning the "Street of the Monks" had acquired its name.[1] However Mr H. G. Ramm, writing for the Archaeological Journal in 1968 stated his theory that, the street called Monkgate we know today, was not, he believed laid out until the 11th or 12th century. Until then the main route into York from Monk Bridge was the ancient right of way, Groves Lane, which led from this bridge across the Groves area to Lord Mayor's Walk. The entrance of this lane in Lord Mayor's Walk stood opposite the old Roman gateway, called the Porta Decumana, which lay south of the present Monk Bar. The road from this gate led directly to the Minster. In Pre Conquest times the Minster was referred to as a Monasterium and the clergy as Monks. Thus Mr Ramm stated that Groves Lane could have been the original Monkgate. When the area around the old St. Maurice's Church was developed and new houses built near there, called Newbiggin, a new thoroughfare was laid out, leading from a new gateway, possibly built with stones from the old Roman gateway in Lord Mayor's Walk. This new gate and bar was called Monk Bar and the new road was given the name of the old right of way, Monkgate. There was also another right of way, which now goes by the name, Love Lane and led from the Foss at Monk Bridge to Barker Hill, now St. Maurice's Road. According to Mr Ramm, this lane could have led to another postern gate by the Merchant Taylor's Hall and then on to St. Andrewgate. More credence is given to these theories by the fact that the old church St. John Del Pyke, meaning the church next to the gate, once stood next to the Porta Decumana and another old church, St. Helen on the Walls, stood next to a gateway in Barker Hill.[2]

Some Roman remains have been found in the Monkgate, Lord Mayor's Walk areas. In 1842, whilst excavating a cellar north west of Monk Bar, a skeleton, fragments of pottery, a jet finger ring and a circular perfume box were found. Roman pottery was also found in the area of Lord Mayor's Walk and Huntington Road. In 1833, a small Roman cemetery was discovered in a field near the junction of Wigginton and Haxby Roads. There were a dozen burials and some Roman pottery found there. A stone coffin containing a skeleton was found in 1839 on the west side of Clarence Street.[3]

Drake found that there had been people owning land and living in Monkgate in the years following the Norman Conquest. Some of these left gifts of their lands to St. Mary's Abbey. King William the Conqueror gave St. Mary's "One Caracate of land in Monkgate" Roger, son of Bernulf granted land "where on he dwelt in

MONKGATE 1820's.

Monkgate and Bar. Showing entrance to Old St. Maurice's Church c.1840 (*City of York Council*)

Monkgate". Alice, daughter of Richard Grafey and late wife of Hamo Le Gaunt "all her land in Monkgate". Michael de Roumangour and Gundrela gave "two tofts in Newbiggin Street". Elyas Flour, son of William de Merkington, granted "all his lands in which he had in the suburbs of York in Newbiggin".[4]

Monk Bar

Monk Bar, like the Bars at Micklegate and Walmgate were probably at first no more than an entrance through the simple defences of the Roman town, Eboracum. When the new road, Monkgate was laid out sometime in the 12th century this gate became more important. It was originally called Monkgate Bar and was the strongest of the medieval gateways. It was built as a self contained fortress with every floor defensible even if the other floors were captured. The lower three storeys were vaulted in stone and were fireproof. The super structure which rises higher than the other Bars was erected during the 14th century. The two outer angles of this Bar are capped by half length human figures, probably 17th century replacements of earlier carvings, in the act of hurling down stones. This was supposed to act as a deterrent to would be invaders. Above the central arch are two rooms, leased in the 15th century as a dwelling house and in the 16th used as a prison. One of the little rooms in the turrets was known as the "Little Ease" and it was in here that Roman Catholic recusants and other offenders were confined. Above these rooms is a chamber containing the hoisting equipment of the portcullis, the only one that has survived in York. This Bar was repaired in 1825 when the Barbican was removed and side arches were added. The guard house, which stood next to the Bar was demolished at this time also. The larger archway was widened in 1861 to allow hay carts to enter the City. The Bar was restored by the Corporation in the 1950's.[5]

In 1606, a man entering the city via Bootham Bar was not omitted by the watchman but sent to Monk Bar. He needed a midwife for his wife who was in labour. In 1607, a man was detained in the prison for uttering opprobrious words against the Lord Mayor.[6] The gates to the Bars were locked at dusk and manned by guards who often refused people entrance especially in times of plague. In 1660, John Wightman, miller at Monk Bar, "his house was shut up as his father had laid there and his Mother had died at Osbaldwick of the plague the night after".[7] In the 16th century, a man who lived in Petergate had been playing cards with his friends who lived outside Layerthorpe Postern. When he tried to get back to his house he found that Monkgate Bar was locked. However on looking for the guards he found them all drunk and asleep in the upper room. He and his friends stole the keys from the guards and opened the gates of the Bar and returned safely to Petergate.[8]

Paynelath's Crofts

The Groves is an area bounded by Huntington Road, Monkgate, Lord Mayor's Walk, Clarence Street and Haxby Road. It was once known as Paynelaths,

Monk Bar. (Etty) *(City of York Council)*

Paynele's or Pealey's Crofts. Laths is an Anglo Saxon name for barns, so it could mean the barns and fields of Payne. The name survives today in Penley's Grove Street. This area lay in the medieval parish of St. Maurice and most of the land before the 16th century was owned by St. Mary's Abbey. Part of the land was enclosed and made into closes or crofts at this time. At the north east limit of the area, on rising ground, stood a windmill belonging to the Abbey and below this on the River Foss were three water mills.[9]

In 1624, William Peacock of York left to his wife, "All myne interest which I have in the Abbey Mills alias Foss Mills and one windmill in Payneles Crofts".[10] The Abbey windmill stood on Mill Hill which was at the end of the present Groves Terrace. These mills are often mentioned in medieval documents. In medieval times the boundaries in Bootham and Gillygate were constantly being disputed. An agreement in 1354, gave St. Mary's Abbey access along Gillygate to Paynelath's Crofts, which lay between the north eastern city wall and the River Foss. The city only succeeded in bringing Paynelath's Crofts within the boundary of its common lands in the 16th century.[11] In 1558, in the City records, there is a mention of a muster of soldiers held on the Crofts and in 1576, Edward Fawcett was ordered, to make a ditch at the far end of Paynelathe's Crofts. East of Monkgate, St. Maurice's Parish of 1852, extended into Jewbury and into a small area, now occupied by the Gas Works, that had once belonged to the Vicar's Choral, called Vicar's Lees.[12]

Newbiggin

Outside the city walls there was a lot of development in the 11th and 12th centuries. There were early settlements in Bootham and Clementhorpe and a ribbon development outside Walmgate Bar. There were also buildings in Gillygate on a garden once used by the inmates of St. Leonard's Hospital. Outside Monkgate there are records of early settlements between Monkgate and Layerthorpe Postern. By 1200, there was limited development in Lord Mayor's Walk, adjacent to the old St. Maurice's Church, called Newbiggin, meaning new buildings.[13] In 1361, there is a mention in old deeds, of a tenement and croft in Newbiggin, owned by John Treboys, which he left to the Guild of Jesus Christ. In the 15th century, John Raskelf also had a tenement in Newbiggin, next to St. Maurice's church.[14]

Old St. Maurice's Church

There has been a church dedicated to St. Maurice on a site at the corner of Monkgate and Lord Mayor's Walk from early times. A medieval document dated between 1195 and 1210 mentions this church, but it could have been erected even earlier. It was once in the possession of the Dean and Chapter of York

Old St. Maurice's Church. This Church was demolished in the 1870's and a new Church built. *(Courtesy of Mr M. Powell)*

Minster. This church was a small building comprising, a nave with a south aisle, chancel, south porch and vestry. A small wooden bell turret surmounted the roof of the nave. In the 16th century this church like many other city churches was in a state of decay. In 1586 it was, along with the old church of St. John del Pyke, joined to Holy Trinity Church, Goodramgate. John del Pyke was later demolished but St. Maurice survived. It received a lot of damage in the Civil War along with some houses in Monkgate but was repaired then and seemed to have been rebuilt piecemeal at all periods.

In 1428, John Raskelf paid 6d per annum for the maintenance of a lamp and for masses said for Robert Holme and his relatives. In 1704 Joyce Holtby left money for this church and the poor of the parish and in 1708 this church received some money willed by John and Elizabeth Clapham towards its upkeep and repair.[15] Through the years wealthy men and women have bequeathed similar gifts of money to the poor of the parish and to supplement the stipend of the Vicar of St. Maurice. In early times the churchyard of this church projected into Monkgate and made this road very narrow. The Corporation demolished part of the churchyard in the 1850's to make the road wider. In 1872, when a new church was needed, the vicar of St. Maurice, Rev. Gilchrist-Wilson, sought compensation from York Corporation, claiming the churchyard had been altered without the permission of the Archbishop.[16]

Lord Mayor's Walk

Lord Mayor's Walk, formerly known as Goose Lane, ran from Monkgate to Gillygate, outside the moat of the city walls. Goose Lane was mentioned in records as early as the 14th century but it was only a rough track. In 1576, the City Chamberlaines were ordered to pave Goose Lane. "So men may pass to Paynelaths's Crofts". A name for the City Moat that lay next to the Walls was the Goosedyke. In 1447, there was an entry in the Bridgemaster's Rolls, for 12d received from John Raskelf and William Preston, owners of tenements which lay towards the Goosedyke. Access to Paynelath's Crofts was by Shoter or Shouter lane, an ancient right of way, now known as Groves Lane, which once crossed the Groves area from Lord Mayor's Walk to Lowther Street.[17] In a deed of 1708, a house not far from Monk Bar, looking towards the Pealey Crofts was mentioned. In 1731 there is a record of a lease of a farm with closes called Cuckow Nest which adjoined Groves Lane.[18] In 1742, John Dalton was fined £5 for cutting down Ash trees in Monk Bar moat.[19] Lord Mayor's Walk at this time was a wide thoroughfare lined with Elms on both sides.[20]

St. Maurice's Road

This road that now leads from Monkgate to Layerthorpe Bridge was known as Barker Hill in medieval times, as there were tanning works here and it was once the home of parchment and leather workers. Barker Hill went by the name of Harlot Hill as well and Drake commented in his book on York that the name was

Aerial view of old houses in Layerthorpe (demolished in 1930's) Foss Bank, Gas Works, County Hospital, Bar Walls and St. Maurice's Road (Courtesy of Mr M. Powell)

not given for nothing. However the name "harlot" was used to mean a beggar or vagabond in medieval times, so it was probably the area outside the city walls where food was left for beggars. The skins from the tanning works were washed in the Foss. In 1576, York Corporation laid down laws, which stated that "No tanner or parchment maker should wash skins in the Foss, where men should fetch water to drink". From Barker Hill, a right of way ran through the fields to the Foss Bank, near Monk Bridge called Love Lane. This lane was described in the 13th. Century records as a common path by the fields of Monkgate and was known in 1478 as Jewbury Lane, as it crossed the area used by the Jews as a cemetery. It acquired its present name in the 19th. Century.[21]

Jewbury

The Jewish community in York was well established by 1170. Latin sources indicate that the prosperity of the Jews in York was mainly derived from providing loans to Yorkshire landowners. A few individuals, such as Aaron of York, achieved national standing and became a financier to the Crown. Tradition has it that a loan from him financed the making of the "Five Sisters" window in the Minster. Although the most famous episode in the history of the Jews in York was the massacre in Clifford's Tower in 1190, this was not the end of the York community, which enjoyed its greatest prosperity in the first half of the 13th century. It is not known exactly what date the Jewish cemetery in York was established, but in 1177 the Crown allowed Jews to purchase land outside the walls of cities for use as cemeteries. It was important that the area which was used for this purpose was still rural as this conformed to Jewish law. Sometime in the 12th century, the Jews bought land at the bottom of Barker Hill, now called, St. Maurice's Road, and established a cemetery. The cemetery would need a washhouse for the ritual washing of the bodies before burial. Sometimes there were separate burial areas for men, women and children. Tombstones were often erected but no evidence was found of any in the York cemetery. It may have been planted with trees and shrubs and enclosed with walls as a protection against vandalism. A Jewish cemetery was often described in the records as a Jewish garden.[22]

By 1290 the Jews were all expelled from England and all their property was claimed by the Crown. The cemetery in York together with a house and eight selions of land were valued at £1 per annum and sold to Robert de Newland, a tanner of York and Alice Gisburn his wife. After Robert's death in 1301, the property was sold to Thomas de Stodley, citizen of York who had acquired substantial properties in the Monkgate area. "Alice de Gysburne, widow of Robert de Newland, tanner of York, to Thomas de Stodelay of York, land called le Jubyri and other lands with buildings outside le Jubyri in Barkergate, which she has from the gift of the king". Later the estate was acquired by the Clervaux family of Croft, who remained the landlords for the next two centuries.[23]

In 1829, when Layerthorpe Postern was demolished, a Jewish amulet was discovered. Bodies were often laid out in a room in the Postern before being taken to the cemetery.[24] By the 1850's the area near the cemetery was built up with terrace housing, Orchard Street and Jewbury. These houses were demolished in the 1960s and now it is the site of Sainsbury's car park, who have erected a plaque to show that it was once the burial ground of the Jews.[25]

Haxby Road

Haxby Road bore the name Pepper Mill Lane in early times. The name was derived from the windmill which stood near the entrance to the now Fountayne Street. This windmill was mentioned in the Clifton Book of Records. It was occupied by the Randerson family for many years. At the junction of the two roads near the end of Clarence Street there once stood the gallows belonging to the Dean and Chapter of York Minster. It administered justice in its own jurisdiction of Peter Prison up to 1835 when it passed into the hands of the Judges and Assizes.

The Horse Fair

In Medieval times, in this same area was a large tract of land called the Horse Fair, the site of many of the annual fairs. Two roads went through the Horse Fair, one from Wigginton, known then as the road from Clifton and one from Huntington now known as Haxby Road. The heavy wains from the fields in Clifton and the carts from Huntington used to churn up the end of Clarence

Clarence Street c. 1900. *(W. Hayes)*

Street, There were numerous complaints in the city records of the state of this road. There were two bridges in this area also, one called the Forest Bridge, which was the farthest away from the city. The other bridge was called the Cow Bridge and marked on the 1850 OS map as standing near the present District Hospital. There were several ponds in the Horse fair one called the Great Pond. These together with the ditches, were scoured out from time to time. A plague lodge was built in the Horse Fair during the great visitations of the plague in 1603 and 1605 when over 3,000 people died in York.

St. Mary's Hospital

Near the entrance of Union Terrace, once stood a hospital founded by the Dean of York in 1314 and dedicated to St. Mary Magdalene. A Master or Chaplain was to celebrate Divine Service daily with two chaplains to pray for certain people and all Christian souls. The two chaplains were to have victuals and clothes or 24 Shillings yearly instead of clothes. Six old and infirm chaplains unable to perform services were to be maintained. The house and chapel were surrounded by a wall and in 1416 there was a mention of an old oak tree standing near the Great Gate. After the Dissolution this hospital remained empty for many years. The buildings were finally granted to the Dean and Chapter to form the headquarters of their ancient grammar school of St. Peter's. The school remained here until 1644 when the buildings were burnt in the siege of York.[26]

Monk Bridge

The bridge over the River Foss at the bottom end of Monkgate was always known as Monk Bridge. Little is known of its early history but in medieval times it had three arches. A small leper hospital dedicated to St. Loy once stood near the bridge. In 1428, an inmate of this hospital, William Manying had made a will. He left ½ lb of wax to be burnt around his body and 6d to York Minster and the residue to his wife, Agnes. When the old Woodman Inn was demolished in the 1920's to widen this bridge, the remains of a small leper hospital were discovered.[27]

In 1518, there is a reference to a garden at the east end of the bridge and a mention of "Walking there at pleasure". Another record of 1582 stated that "Alderman May laid in pain (was fined) because he had not paved before his orchard near Monk Bridge and had not taken up stones which had fallen there".[28] Monk Bridge was purposely demolished in 1644 as a means of preventing the Parliamentary army entering the City. It had a temporary wooden crossing afterwards for fifteen years until it was rebuilt. In 1794, during work on repairing this bridge, the central arch collapsed killing two workmen, J Wood and Thomas Day. A sum of £20 was paid by York Corporation to their widows.[29]

Maison Dieu of Robert Holme

No remains have been found of the numerous Maisons Dieu or houses of God that have been recorded in early deeds of York. The founder of the Monkgate Maison Dieu was probably Robert Holme. He came to York from Holme on the Wolds and served the city as a chamberlain in 1352 and mayor in 1368. He gained possession of a house near Monk Bridge and converted it into a home with twenty beds for invalids of both sexes. In his will, he instructed his son Robert and his heirs to uphold and keep it in good condition. One English penny was to be paid for every poor person occupying a bed every day of every year, for a hundred years. His descendants seem to have carried out the terms of the will and in 1402, Thomas de Howam left 10 shillings to the poor in the hospital in Monkgate. After the Reformation, Thomas Holme of Elvington, gentleman, sold property in Monkgate described as "one cottage called Le Maison Dieu with a garth adjoining".

Monk Bridge. c.1790. *(City of York Council)*

Chapter I. Notes and References.
1. Drake, Francis. *The History of the Antiquities of York*. (1736) bk. 1. pp. 254. 255.
2. Ramm, H.G. *Notes on Archaeological Finds*. in Y.A.J. Vol. 42 (1968) pp. 133-135.
3. Royal Commission For Historic Monuments. London. *Eboracum*. Burials. pp. 71. 72.
4. Op. cit. 1. Drake. p. 583.
5. Royal Commission for Historic Monuments.(London) *City of York*. vol 11, *The Defences*. pp. 125, 129-135
6. York City Archives (subsequently referred to as Y.C.A.). *York City House Books*. XXXIII 50. 86.
7. Osbaldwick History Group. *History of Osbaldwick*. Smith. (1980) p.44.
8. White, E. *Elizabethan York*. Y.A.Y.A. Maxiprint. P. 25.
9. Raine, A. *Medieval York*. J. Murray (1955) p. 280.281.
10. Y.C.A. Deed. E127.
11. Op. cit. 9. Raine. pp. 280. 281.
12. Y.C.A. B/Y 63b. (1428) B/Y 11d. (1361).
13. P.M. Tillot(ed) Victoria County History. *City of York*. (Subsequently referred to as V.C.H.) p. 395.
14. Y.C.A. B/Y 63b 1428.
15. V.C.H. pp. 394. 395. 430.
16. Y.R.L. y942.741 Correspondence between Vicar of St. Maurice and Town Clerk. 1872.
17. Op. cit. 9. Raine. p. 279.
18. Y.C.A. *G. Leeman's Deeds*. Acc. 22/2vc.
19. Y.C.A. B43/86.
20. Drake. p. 254.
21. Raine. p. 282.
22. King's Manor Library. Lilley, JM & others. The Archaeology of York. *The Jewish Burial Ground at Jewbury*. pp. 301-3. 305.
23. N.Y.R.O. Clervaux. Cartulary. Folios 96v 97. 1291. 1336.
24. Raine. p. 282.
25. Y.C.A. Demolition Papers. Jewbury. Lower Orchard St. 1960.
26. Raine. pp. 271-275.
27. Ibid p. 284.
28. Y.C.A. 1518 B/9/96. 1518. E31/180 1582.
29. Y. Courant, 8 Dec. 1794.
30. Raine. p. 283.

CHAPTER II

LIFE IN GEORGIAN AND VICTORIAN TIMES

Monk Bar c. 1900 *(W. Hayes)*

Church Wardens' Accounts

The church wardens' accounts for the Church of St. Maurice in the early 19th century give us a little insight into the lives of some of the people living in that parish. In a vestry meeting of 1797 we see who were the prominent people. William Lund was paid £5 per annum for collecting the taxes when James Richardson was the vicar. Other men attending that meeting were J lamb, J Rowntree, H Briggs and Matthew Bottrill (George Hudson's uncle) Other names mentioned at another meeting were W. Walker, D. Peacock, Robert Young Bearpark and William Bell. All these men would have some standing in the parish at this time.

At a meeting of the Overseers of the Poor, held in 1801, when M. Weaver and John Wardell were the churchwardens, an application was considered for the family of John Brown who had fallen on hard times. In 1806, when James Dallin was the vicar, J. Monkman and T. Smith were recorded as churchwardens, Robert Bewlay and James Benson were also mentioned.

In the accounts for the year 1857, we see that Mr Henry Bowman was paid for supplying coals to the church. There were also accounts for work done by Mr Jackson, glazier, Mr Fawdington, joiner, and Mr Knowles, painter. All these men would be local tradesmen. At this meeting it was noted that a rent of £9 18s was received for a close at Bishopthorpe and 10s given to the Grey Coat School. The names of Elizabeth Rawdon and Mr Henry Othic were also mentioned and Mr T Ellis was said to be the clerk.[1]

Below is a selection of extracts from the Church wardens' accounts from St. Thomas's Church when the vicar was the Rev. Sampson.

1854.

Mr John Smith for playing the harmonium and teaching the choir. Paid 18 shillings

1859.

Blind boy playing the harmonium. 5 Shillings. Mr Lucas, stonemason. Paid £1.

1866.

J Pulleyn, 15 Shillings, Hibbert, glazier and painter, 18s.6d. Mr Hopwood, organist. 18 Shillings.

1881.

Mr Joseph Volans, joiner, £3 for new floor. G Richardson, gardener mowing grass. 5 Shillings. J Saville, bottle of port wine. 2s.11d. R Charlesworth, choirmaster. Coultas and Volans, printer. Mrs Sidwell, sextoness.

1884

John Lane, coke and chips for firewood, £1.10.11d. Mr Arthur Lawson, bell ringer and organ blower £1.2.6d. W H Thackray, $^1/_2$ dozen bottles of port wine.

1895.

R Fowler, bell ringer £1.2.6d. Paid the Industrial School 5 Shillings for firewood for church.[2]

Pew Rents

In early times parishioners paid to sit in certain pews in the church at Sunday services. Which was a way of raising money. There was competition to sit in the best seats. In 1821, in the records for St. Maurice, there are accounts of a Mr Buckle who had sat in one of the best pews in the gallery, instead of part of a pew belonging to a Mr Harrison. Tenants of Mr Robert Cattle of Grove House were permitted to sit in the first pews. Mr Clapham's family and servants and Mr Dawson's wife and servants were allowed to sit in a pew in the Gallery provided that £20 a year was paid to the upkeep of the church. Mr Hopwood had to pay £5 for the use of his pew.[3]

Bowman Family

James Bowman was first mentioned in the 1840, as living at number 1 Monkgate. This would be under the Bar. He was listed as a coal merchant and had a yard just at the side of the Bar (Monk Bar court) Later his son lived

Bowman's Removal Firm. Monkgate c. 1900

there and was a wheelwright and joiner. Thomas Bowman furniture remover was recorded as living in St. Maurice's Road in the 1840's, but shortly after moved to Monkgate. The removal firm of T Bowman, later to become James Bowman and Sons, was established in Mongate in the 1840's, when it advertised its new system of removing furniture taking all risks. In the early years of the 20th century there were premises to store furniture along St. Maurice's Road and also on both sides of Monkgate. Auctions were held periodically to sell the unwanted stock. The business passed down through six generations and finally closed in the 1970's. Mr James Bowman was the proprietor of the firm and Conservative Councillor for Monk Ward in 1949. His son Philip was also a councillor, 1968 to 1971.[4]

William Scawin

In Victorian times many rich and important men of the city lived in Monkgate. William Scawin lived at No. 31, just two doors away from the Black Horse public house. He was a chemist, druggist and tea dealer and had a shop at the corner of Goodramgate and Petergate. He became a freeman of the city and served as a churchwarden at Christ Church, King's Square. He was once described as "a little man with sharp outlined features and dressed in the costume of the 18th century, that is a coat without a turned down collar, a vest and knee breeches of black cloth, black stockings and low shoes and a white neckerchief around his neck".[5]

St. Maurices Church and Monkgate c. 1900

In 1839 he retired from business in favour of his son, William Scawin junior and Richard Dresser. The firm then became known as Scawin and Dresser. By strict attention to business and rigid economy, William Scawin amassed a large fortune, which he apportioned to his sons and daughters. After his death, he bequeathed a sum of £1000 for the restoration of Christ Church, which was then in a dilapidated state, on condition that he was buried there near his wife. He owned property in Colliergate, Petergate, Heworth, Fulford and Clifton.

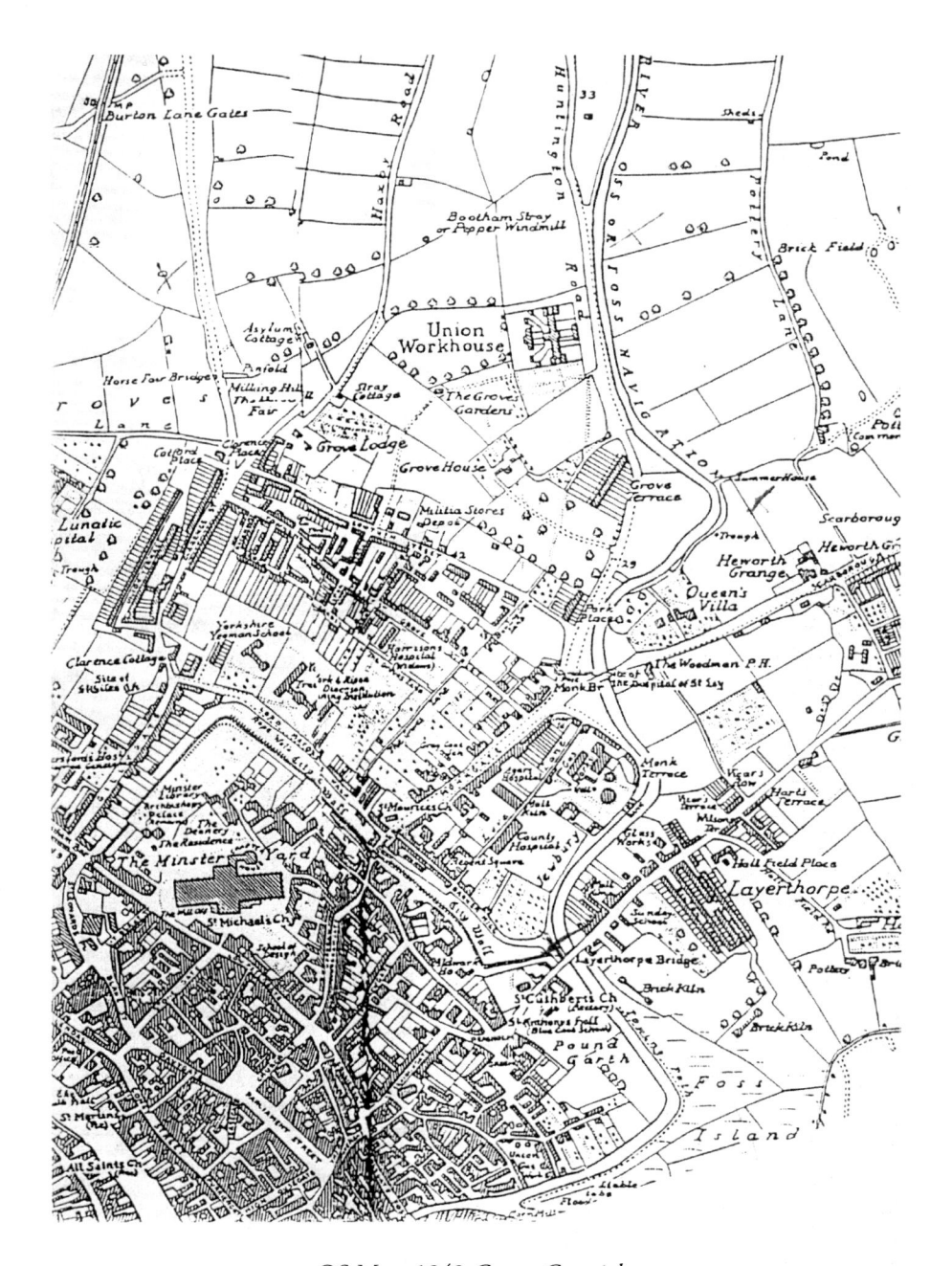

OS Map. 1849 *Crown Copyright*

He also had a farm at Barton Hill, Spittle Bridge and Acklam and houses at Scarborough and Redcar. He received a substantial income from all these properties. He also owned and leased out another house in Monkgate, No. 21, to a Mrs Reed. He had stocks and shares in the Great Western and the Great Eastern railways. All his monthly income and expenditure was meticulously recorded in numerous ledgers, many of which have survived and enables us an insight into the financial affairs of a rich Victorian gentleman. He died in 1866, and was buried in York cemetery and not in Christ Church as he wished.[6]

Grove House

This house was built in the early years of the 19th century. It stood in large grounds off Huntington Road, somewhere at the end of the present Brownlow Street. It was built for Mr Robert (Dobbin) Cattle who died there in 1842. Mr Cattle, who was born at Sheriff Hutton, was originally a York Silversmith. He later entered into a partnership with a Mr Maddocks and owned the stables attached to the York Tavern in St. Helen's Square, that supplied horses for the mail coaches.[7] The original estate that surrounded Grove House had been bought by Mr Cattle for £10,500 and consisted of sixty acres of land, forty acres of meadow and forty acres of pasture for cattle. It stretched from Huntington Road to Haxby Road. By the 1820's Mr Cattle had begun to sell some of this land.[8]

In the 1880's, after the death of Mr Luke Thompson, solicitor, who was the last occupant, this house and the estate was put up for auction. It was described as a well built dwelling house with stables, coach house, conservatory, vinery, flower and vegetable gardens and a large orchard. The house had a dining room, drawing room and a morning room on the ground floor. There were seven bedrooms and a dressing room on the next floor and attic bedrooms for servants. Several acres of grassland and pasture adjoined the house. Some of the estate had already been sold for building purposes. A portion of the estate had been sold previously to the York School Board and a school was in the process of erection. No trace of this house now remains.[9]

Eliza Tabor

Eliza Tabor was born in York in 1835, into a staunch Methodist family. Her father, John Tabor, opened a private school for boys at No.5 Penley's Grove Street, also called Grove House. This was a large detached house with coach house, stables, a large lawn and circular drive.

When Eliza was 21, she fell in love with a man of Anglican faith. In her day, the "mixed marriage" between a Methodist and an Anglican would have been unthinkable, consequently when Eliza's betrothed refused to become a Methodist she broke off the engagement and spent the next twenty years helping her father at his school in the Groves. It was at this time that she began to write novels, putting into her books all her personal heartbreak and suffering caused by the conflict between the Church of England and the Methodist Church. At the age of thirty eight she met and married a widower with three children and spent the remainder of her life fully occupied and happy.

John Tabor's house changed its name to Settrington House in the 1890's and in the 1920's became part of Groves Working Men's Club.

Eliza Tabor's novels, which were originally published anonymously, although full of Victorian sentiment, paint a vivid picture of the religious beliefs of Victorian York and so are of great social significance.[10]

The Hirstwood Family

In April 1839, an advertisement appeared in the Yorkshire Gazette stating that pottery kilns and a warehouse were to be erected in the Groves area for the manufacture, gilding and burnishing of china by a Mr Hirstwood of Stonegate. This had never been attempted in the city before. Mr Haigh Hirstwood came to York in the late 1820's to open a shop for the Bramelds, selling china and cut glass. This shop was at first in the Masonic Hall, Little Blake Street, it later moved to Coney Street. Mr Hirstwood had previously been employed at the Rockingham China Works near Rotherham, under the Bramelds, and described as a clever painter of flowers and insects. He and his sons, Joseph and Thomas, had once been engaged upon decorating the dessert services of William IV and the Duchess of Cumberland.

In the 1830's, Haigh Hirstwood branched out on his own and opened a china shop in Stonegate. He also bought land in Lowther Street, near to the present church of St. Thomas, to build a warehouse and kilns to burnish and decorate plain white china. He was assisted by his son in law, William Leyland, who had married his daughter, Mary, in 1828. Leyland had also worked under the Bramelds and was said to be a good painter, gilder and enameller also. However disagreements arose and the partnership was dissolved. The works in Lowther Street continued until 1850.

Haigh Hirstwood's other daughter Sarah, married William Hoyle, a school teacher and they later opened a glass and china shop, at first in Parliament Street then at 12, St. Sampson Square. Sarah's eldest daughter, Mary Anne had a baby linen shop. Eliza Jane Hirstwood, granddaughter to Haigh Hirstwood, married William Eskett, photographer, in 1867. They had a studio in Lendal near where Bank's music shop is now, and they lived in Garden Street in the Groves.

Haigh Hirstwood died in 1854 but his son William carried on the business in Coney street. His grandson, another William, was also in the same trade but only sold the china and cut glass.[11]

The New Workhouse

In January 1849, a new workhouse was erected on a site along Huntington Road. The old workhouse had been in Marygate. The new building built by

Workhouse, Huntington Road, built 1849. *(Courtesy of Y.R.L.)*

Penty and Penty was still a grim and forbidding place. Men and women were still segregated. There were separate wards for men, boys, idiots and vagrants as well as an Industrial School for boys. The women had their own wards, yards and lying in rooms, with dormitories for infants and girls under nine. There was also a general infirmary, and wards for fever and infectious diseases.(12) In 1900 conditions in the Workhouse were still very bad. A report by the Board of Guardians stated that the inmates were only served potatoes that were black and soapy. There was also a problem with the meat that was badly carved into chunks, meaning some people would only get fat and those with bad teeth could not chew it. The food was not fit to be put in front of a human being the report concluded. When the Board tried to get to the bottom of what had gone wrong, all the committees involved with the running of the Workhouse blamed each other for the sad state of affairs.[13]

Ann Harrison's Hospital

This hospital or Home, known locally as the "Old Maid's Home" which stood on a site at the corner of Penley's Grove Street and St. John's Crescent, was founded by Anne Harrison in 1845 to provide homes for eight poor women, widows or spinsters. This lady conveyed two acres of land in the Groves area to ten trustees and under her will left £7,000 of which £1,200 was allotted to cover the cost of erecting a hospital in her memory, the remainder to provide a pension of £20 a year to each inmate. The foundation stone of the hospital was laid on the 25th October 1845. Stone busts of the foundress and her husband

Ann Harrison's Hospital, Penley's Grove Street. Demolished 1960's.
(Courtesy of Y.C.A.)

adorned the hospital walls and life size portraits were erected in the rooms. In the 1960's this Home was in a bad state of repair and the chapel had not been used in years. Along with many of the small houses in Penley's Grove Street this Home was demolished and Grove House, a residential home for the elderly was built in its place.[14]

Thomas Agar's Hospital

This comprised of three cottages built in the 17th century near to the present Agar Street in Monkgate. The charity was established in 1631 by Thomas Agar, for six poor widows. By the 19th century the buildings were extremely dilapidated and were finally closed in 1879. The cottages were replaced by a pension charity and in 1956 five pensioners each received £8.

The County Hospital

The work of caring for the sick was nobly performed by St. Leonard's Hospital and other smaller almshouses until 1539 when the monasteries and their hospitals were all dissolved by Henry VIII. For the next two hundred years, the suffering and the afflicted had to depend on scant private aid. In 1740, Lady Elizabeth Hastings bequeathed £500 for the relief of the diseased poor in York. This fund was augmented by donations from other charitably minded people and a hospital in the modern sense was established in Monkgate for medical

Children's Ward, York County Hospital. 1930.

treatment and nursing care. For some time this hospital was the only one of its kind north of the Trent. The original building stood close to the roadway of Monkgate on a site immediately in front of the present hospital. The frontage of this building was 75ft. by 35ft. It had three floors. On the first floor were offices, on the second, two large wards, male and female and on the third, two more wards and an operating theatre. Every ward had a necessary house from which care was taken to remove offensive smells and much care was given to cleanliness. There was a garden at the back were cows were kept to supply milk for the hospital.[16]

The new hospital was built in the 1850's. It stood further back from the main road than the previous one. In 1865, a list of required behaviour for patients and visitors was drawn up. There was to be no gambling, spitting, smoking or vandalism on the wards. There was to be no mixing of male and female patients. Sitting on the sides of the beds or lying on the beds with shoes on was not permitted. Patients were not allowed to stay up after 9pm in winter or 9:30pm in summer.

Much of the hospital's income at this time came from subscriptions made to the hospital from the gentry and well to do York businessmen. One such subscriber was Rosalind, Lady Carlisle, of Castle Howard. In 1890 she had made a bed available at the gatehouse at Castle Howard for hospital patients to convalesce. However she had complained to the Hospital Board that one such patient had died of Typhoid fever. She disagreed with the hospital's policy of mixing fever patients with others and subsequently withdrew her subscription.

In the 18th and 19th centuries hospitals were not very pleasant places. Medical patients were mixed with surgical and infectious diseases could spread very quickly. The burial registers of St. Maurice showed that in the early 19th century, one third of all burials were from the hospital. Between 1820 and 1830 over a thousand leeches had been used for treatment. This practice declined a little in the latter part of the century.[17]

Chapter II. Notes and References.
1. Borthwick Institute of Historical Research. Y/St. Mau. *Church Warden's Accounts.* (1797. 1801. 1857).
2. Borthwick. Y/St. Thomas. *Church Wardens Accounts.*
3. Op. cit. 1. (1821).
4. Murray, H. *Pedigrees of York Families.*
5. Y.R.L. Article on William Scawin. Knowles. *Notes on Goodramgate.*
6. Y.C.A. *Scawin family papers.* AC 135 Box 19.20.
7. Y.R.L. *York Cuttings Book.* 1852-91 p.278.
8. Y.C.A. *Abstract of Title of Mr R. Cattle to Grove House* in (C.P.O. 1957) Box 2377. Lowther St.
9. Y.R.L. Yorks. Gazette. 3-7-1886.
10. Y.E.P. 13-11-1965.
11. Information supplied by Mrs Patsy Hirstwood, Tostig Avenue, York.
12. V.C.H p.468.
13. Y.E.P. June 1900.
14. V.C.H. p.426.
15. Ibid p.423.
16. Knight, C.B. *History of York.* Herald Printers. (1944) p.532.
17. Borthwick. Y.C. *Hospital Governors Minute Books* 1820-1890.

B. J. Covell, Bootmaker, c1900. Corner of Park Grove and Diamond Street.
(Courtesy of A. Blincoe)

CHAPTER III
HOUSING DEVELOPMENT

Early Houses

The oldest houses in this area are in Monkgate. There are records of people living in this area in medieval times. There were also some early houses just outside Monk Bar, near St. Maurice's Church, called Newbiggin or new buildings. Many of the houses near the Bar were destroyed in the Civil War. The first houses in Penley's Grove Street date from the 1830's. Most of the other streets developed as more working class houses were needed for workers for the Railway and later for Rowntree's factory when it was built in Haxby Road. These houses had to be within walking distance of the places of employment.[1]

Monkgate Houses

No 38 Monkgate was called Middleton House and built about 1700 for Benjamin West who owned the two adjoining tenements. Subsequent owners were Issac Johnson, a baker and in 1772, Joseph Beckett, silk weaver. In 1774, in a sale by the widow of a later owner, John Preston, two newly built chambers over the carriageway were mentioned. In 1798, the house was bought by Reverend Charles Wellbeloved, an antiquarian and Principal of Manchester College, which was founded in Manchester for dissenters, Unitarians etc. In 1811, the College moved to York to Wellbeloved's house. The house was then enlarged and extended on the ground floor.

Number 42, was acquired by George Hudson in 1828 and No. 44 was built by Robert Edwards, yeoman in 1723. Two earlier houses which had been on this site had been destroyed in the siege of 1644 in the Civil War. No. 44 was leased by John Houghton, gent, between 1741 and 1747 but later became the property of Thomas Beckworth, painter and antiquary. It later passed to George Hudson who altered it to make Nos. 42 and 44 one mansion.[2] In 1847, it was put up for sale. It was described as having on the ground floor, entrance hall, breakfast room, study, kitchen, housekeeper's buttery and servant's rooms. On the first floor there were four drawing rooms, dining room, butler's rooms, two bedrooms and a dressing room. On the second floor there were seven bedrooms, three dressing rooms and a bathroom. There were pipes for hot and cold water, two water closets, servant's quarters and attics. There was also three coach houses and stabling for eight horses.[3]

George Hudson

George Hudson was born at Howsham, a small village not far from Malton, Yorkshire. He was born into a farming family, but did not show any interest in farming so he was apprenticed to a shopkeeper in College Street, Nicholson

Monkgate, showing George Hudson's House.

and Bell, situated then where the National Trust shop is now. In 1821, Hudson married Nicholson's niece, who served in the shop. When Bell retired, the firm became, Nicholson and Hudson. In 1827, Matthew Bottrill, Hudson's great-uncle died, leaving him the bulk of his fortune. Hudson left his rooms over the shop and moved to his house in Monkgate, Nos. 42 and 44. With money to invest he became more of a speculator than a tradesman. York at that time offered certain opportunities for investment and in 1833, Hudson became one of the promoters of the York Union Bank. Hudson was also interested in politics and in 1835 he was elected for Monk Ward and in 1837 became Lord Mayor. However it was not only in politics that Hudson was to make his name. The period between 1830 and 1849 was the age of the great railway boom, when all over England railways were being built. Many of these railways were built to suit the needs of local businessmen and were short lived. George Stephenson, the engineer of the early lines in the north, wanted to have a direct rail link from his native Newcastle to London, passing through the Midlands with their increasing population and heavy industries. Hudson struck up a friendship with Stephenson and eventually managed to make York the focal point of the northern route instead of Leeds. In 1833, Hudson, had been one of a small group of business men who had formed a York Railway Committee and he had been appointed treasurer.[4]

In 1849, by a combination of new promotions, take over bids and doubtful financial jugglery he controlled more than a quarter of the total railway mileage

Monkgate and Monk Bridge. c. 1900

in the country. The heart of this railway empire was York. For twelve years he was virtually the dictator of York and his clique was closely linked on the boards of his various lines and of the York Corporation. He had by this time sold his house in Monkgate and had a country house at Newby Park and a town house in Albert Gate in London. He still kept his finger on the pulse of things in York and in 1846 became Lord Mayor for the third time. During his time as Mayor he was famous for his lavish hospitality and organising gargantuan feasts in the Guildhall. Hudson's empire collapsed in 1849 when some of his more doubtful financial transactions came to light at a meeting of the York and North Midland in the De Grey Rooms. There is no doubt that Hudson gave a much needed boost to York's economy. He not only made York a railway town and lined the pockets of many of his friends and acquaintances, but there was always, contracts for buildings and materials and the York firms who could deliver the goods were always considered first. There was more money in the city and retailers profited accordingly. The number of railway employees rose from forty one in 1841 to five hundred and three in 1851 and by 1855 no less than one thousand were employed in the station and engine works.[5]

William Fawdington

In the 18th century the land near Monk Bridge, Sainsbury's side, was just pasture land. Some of the land at the beginning of Monkgate was owned by John Kilvington and others, and was sold to Timothy Mortimer. In early Victorian times, it was leased to William Cawkill, a seedsman, who had his nurseries here. In 1787, William Fawdington, joiner and carpenter, bought some of this land, called Pinfold Close, from Arabella Mortimer. This close passed down to Thomas Fawdington, son of William, and in 1843, Thomas began to build some of the houses in the parade at the beginning of Monkgate, opposite Penley's Grove Street, now Nos. 70 to 78, previously 1 to 8. It is possible that these houses were not built at the same time. In the 1850 census, William Fawdington, joiner was also listed as the landlord of the Woodman's Inn, near Monk Bridge. His wood yard was behind this Inn. After his death his wife Anne was the licensee of the Woodman Inn.[6]

Bridgend School. Now Brigadier Gerard Public House *(W. Hayes)*

William Hayes

In 1901, the famous Victorian photographer, William Hayes, who was born in St. John Street moved into No. 76 Monkgate at an annual rent of £19 10s. The advantage of this house was that it had a large garden with enough space to build his photographic studio. Mr Hayes probably took the idea of his studio from one in Goodramgate operated by Auguste Mahalaski.

In 1904, William married Margeret Harland from Lastingham, whom he had met at the Temperance Festival at Castle Howard. Both William and his wife were devout Methodists. By 1911, William had decided to move to Hutton le Hole, near Pickering. George Mansfield, William's uncle, who owned the Atlas Works in Layerthorpe and a Mr Kidd, transported the studio intact to the new house in "Beck Garth", Hutton Le Hole.

When Mr Hayes lived in Monkgate he photographed many of his now famous York scenes and numerous ones of Monkgate. He also wrote to his brother Thomas Hayes in 1892 to tell him about the bad floods in York. Bootham,

Marygate and Clifton Green were badly flooded from the River Ouse. The River Foss was also in flood and Layerthorpe, Foss Islands and the Mission Hall, in Mansfield Street, were all affected. The Gas Works flooded and the water from the Foss had flooded Huntington Road as far as the Workhouse.[7]

74 Monkgate

The first occupants recorded living at No. 74, which had been No. 6 before 1861, were Miss Mary and Miss Jane Sampson, relatives of the Rev. Sampson, vicar of St. Thomas. Between 1851 and 1858 Miss Elizabeth Blacker resided here and in 1861 until 1875 this house was occupied by Henry and Eliza Ransley. Mr Ransley was a hairdresser in St. Sampsons' Square. From 1875 until 1881 William Fawdington, junior, son of William Fawdington senior, joiner, and listed as a vetinary surgeon on the 1881 census, appears to have lived at this house. His daughter, Mary, married John Scruton another joiner and from 1881 until 1895 lived at this house with their seven children. One of their children, George William, recorded as a joiner and undertaker, was the next occupant from 1885-89. The Yates family, who owned a confectioner's shop in Petergate, were the occupants in the early 20th century, Mr & Mrs Harold Walker lived there from 1931 until 1973, when Mr & Mrs Powell became the present owners.[8]

Lime Tree School. 62 Monkgate. c.1900 *(Courtesy of Y.R.L.)*

More Monkgate Houses

No. 84, Monkgate, now the public house Brigadier Gerard, was the home of William Banks, timber merchant, in the 1870's. By 1890 it had become a school for boys, Bridgend School. The headmaster in 1900 was Mr W B Lyth. Previously this school had been at number 62 Monkgate. Nos. 62 to 66 are a terrace of three houses built around 1840 by John Shaftoe. Nos. 46 to 48 were built after 1768 for Thomas Beckwith, painter. Miss Cammidge opened her ladies seminary at No. 36 in the 1890's. This school was later called Lime Tree House School and was still in existence in the 1940's, although by then it was at No. 62 Monkgate.[9]

The Bayhorse public house, now called Keystones, was demolished and rebuilt in 1837 by order of the City Council, to conform with the building line. The Icehouse, behind this public house was set into the rampart of the City Wall and was constructed in the early part of the 19th century. It consisted of a circular domed chamber, $12^{1}/_{2}$ feet in diameter, entered by a passage 7 foot long and formerly vaulted. Perishable foods were preserved by means of ice gathered from ponds and streams during the winter months.[10]

Lime Tree House School

Lime Tree House School moved to 62 Monkgate in 1900 and the Head was a Miss Ingleby, who was a quaker. It was a boarding and day school for girls but there was a mixed Kindergarten class.

Lime Tree School. c.1900 *(Courtesy of Y.R.L.)*

Mrs Cynthia Fairclough, née Collins, remembered attending this school in 1940. Miss Ingleby, she recalled was well into her eighties but still taught some of the girls. She was a very good artist and taught them "Barbola" work. She was helped by her cousin, Miss Ireland, a Miss Mann, who lived in the Groves area and a Mrs Nattress, who taught needlework. As there was an average of only eleven or twelve girls in each class, they all received individual attention. There were no boarders in the 1940's and most girls came from "well to do" families, in the York area.

Whilst Mrs Fairclough was a pupil at this school, Miss Ingleby died and the school closed. Mrs Fairclough had to finish her education at Eastern Terrace School, on Heworth Green.[11]

North West Side

In 1846, Nos. 1 to 3 Monkgate were built by James Bowman, coal dealer and wheelwright. They comprised of two houses and shops with a carriage way to the rear. The Black Horse , now the Tap & Spile, was built in the early part of the 19th century. In 1836, when George Wright was the Landlord, it was reported that he had sued a certain Mr Henry Ward, for non payment of a bill. Mr Ward owned an eating house in Davygate. House No. 37, which consisted of three and four storeys, was built for Joseph Buckle in 1848. The fourth storey, to the north east, was a remodelling of an earlier three storey house built by William Walker in 1794.

The houses that are situated from the Monk Chapel to Monk Bridge roundabout were mostly built in the early part of the 19th century. The oldest seems to be No. 55, built by John Mason between 1809 and 1815. It was once the property of the Vicar's Choral. House Nos. 57 and 59 were a three story pair, later converted to a single shop on the ground floor, and were built about 1830. House Nos. 63 to 69, were built by John Hart between 1812 and 1830. No. 69 was occupied by the architect, G.F. Fowler Jones, and built in 1850. House Nos. 71 to 75 were built sometime between 1812 and 1830.[12]

Cuckow Nest

A House and land in Lord Mayor's Walk, near the old St. Maurice's church, were mentioned in a deed of 1673. It was described as "one messuage, (house), one orchard and one close of four acres, in Newbiggin, situated in St. Maurice's parish, without Monkbar, near the walls of the city, for the use of James Tennant, inn holder". In 1770, it was sold to Richard Mann, York gent, described then, as a house or farm known as Cuckow Nest in the occupation of Elizabeth Arden. It was then sold to Thomas Jubb, who passed it down to his grandson Henry Thompson.

Monkgate, showing Monkgate Methodist Chapel *(W. Hayes)*

Bearpark Family

In 1809, some of this land was bought by Robert Young Bearpark from Thompson for £1,150, consisting of a house, yard and outbuildings. The Bearpark family were market gardeners and in the early 19th century, Mr Bearpark lived in a house in Lord Mayor's Walk. This house adjoined the diocesan land whilst the hot houses, greenhouses and propagating frames lay beyond, stretching towards where St. John's Street and Newbiggin Street are now. To the south west there were two closes adjoining Groves Lane, owned by John Raper. Four other gardens, in the area where Garden Street and St. John's Crescent are now, once owned by Henry Edwards, Joseph Marshall and Joseph Webb, were later bought by Robert Bearpark.[13] In 1828, in his will, Robert Young Bearpark left his house and gardens in Lord Mayor's Walk to his son Robert. To his wife Hannah, he left an annuity of £40 a year and all the furniture, china, a clock and a bed with all the hanging sheets, in his house. To his daughter Catherine, he left an annuity and the camp bedstead she slept on and all the bed sheets. The rest of his lands with two garden frames and two glass lights were left to his other son Joseph.[14]

By 1850, the main thorough fare of the Groves, Penley Grove Street and Lowther Street had a network of small streets running between them. There were small courts of cottages leading off Groves Lane and a footpath which branched off it to the end of Garden Street in the vicinity of the Ann Harrison's Almshouses. This footpath was at this time also called Groves Lane but later renamed Garden

Street.[15] Between 1851 and 1871 Robert Bearpark began to sell some of his land for building, St. John Street, Groves Place and Newbiggin Street were the results of these land sales. From the onset the building plots in St. John Street and St. John Crescent were designated for substantial housing, some with attics, whilst those in Groves Place and Newbiggin Street, were built as smaller cottage type dwellings. Some of these cottages occupied a very small area and had no water sanitation. Access to the yard was through the dwelling and some had to share a tap and privy. In 1871, the house and remainder of Mr Bearpark's estate was sold by auction at the Bay Horse, Monkgate. One house, greenhouse, pits, frames and stock in trade.[16]

Speculative Building

Most of the land was sold in small lots to speculators such as Sir James Meek and J Munby, solicitor. Sometimes speculators split their land into smaller and even single lots and sold these to local builders. The builders would often erect a few houses, perhaps living in one themselves and leasing the others. This practice was very profitable to speculators and builders. Terrace housing was cheaper to build than free standing houses and most working class people could only afford to rent. The development of the land in this area progressed for a number of years. James Plummer and John Harper built many of the cottages in Groves Place. James Bowman, Peter Cole, Robert England, James Cartman, William Dennison, George Tinson and Ralf Wheatley were all local builders involved in the construction of properties in this area.

In Victorian times, land in Lower Eldon Street and Lowther Street was owned by Henry Bellerby, bookseller. This land had been bought originally from Robert Cattle in the 1840's. In 1880, Bellerby sold a close called Sixth close or Back Close and another close called Orchard Close to Mr W Chapman. This land adjoined onto premises used as a Depot of the 2nd West York Militia, 84 Lowther Street, later to become the Industrial School.[17] This was in Lowther Street near the church. Many of the properties at the beginning of Lowther Street were constructed by numerous individual builders. This road was described in the Council minutes in 1850 as being "full of pot holes so that no carts could pass". It was described as the worst road at that time in York.[18]

The Castle Howard Ox public house, once called The Castle Howard Fat Ox, was an early Victorian Inn. One of the first Landlords was William Lund, cattle dealer, who obtained his licence in the 1830's.[19]

Houses in Penley's Grove Street were first mentioned in Baines Directories of 1823. Some of the houses, still standing today, were designed by J B and W Atkinson in the 1840's. Most of these had four bedrooms and attics. Some had balconies with anthemion pattern cast-iron railings. At the back of the property was the kitchen, scullery, outhouse and privy. Some had a secondary staircase leading from the kitchen to the servants bedrooms. The original cost of No. 29 was £500, whilst Nos. 35 and 37, being smaller, cost £200 each.[20]

Aerial View from top of gasometer, showing Monk Bridge roundabout
(Courtesy of Mr H Pickard)

Bowling Green Lane

The end of Groves Lane, which leads from Penley's Grove Street, to Lowther Street was always called Bowling Green Lane. At the end of this lane in the early 19th century lay the land of Robert Cattle of Grove House. On a Map made in 1830 a lane leading to a bowling green, which was on Robert Cattle's land, was marked. By 1850 this area had been built on, and had become part of Lowther Street.[21] The Bowling Green Public House was first mentioned in the 1830's as an Inn outside Monk Bar. An early Land Lord, John Hields, was reported to have been discharged insolvent from the York Debtor's Court.[22] In the 1820's Robert Cattle sold some of his land that bordered Huntington Road and built Grove Terrace, these would be some of the first houses to be built in this area. In the 1880's, Mr Luke Thompson, the next owner of Grove house, sold some of his land that bordered Lowther Street, as land for housing, thus Brownlow Street, Princess Street and other streets in that area were laid out. The rest was sold to the Education Board and Park Grove School was then built.

The land that bordered Haxby Road, that had also belonged to Robert Cattle, was sold about the same time and Markham Street and Crescent, Neville Street and other streets in that area were then built. This coincided with the opening of Mr Rowntree's new chocolate works in Haxby Road.[23] A house, called Grove lodge had been in this area in the 1850's. It had been built with materials from the Old Deanery, which it was said to resemble, by Mr Henry Bellerby, bookseller of Stonegate. Later Henry Newton, solicitor, lived there. This house was demolished about 1900 when the area was redeveloped.[24]

Chapter III. Notes and References
1. V.C.H. p. 426.
2. Royal Commission for Historical Monuments. *City of York* p. 89. 90.
3. Y.R.L. Yorks. Gazette. 13-3- 1847.
4. Y.R.L. Lambert, R S *The Railway King.* (1800-1871) pp.268-9. George Hudson.
5. Bailey, B. *The Rise and Fall of the Railway King.* (1995) Sutton. Pp.10. 18. 99-101. 122-123.
6. Information supplied by Mr M. Powell, 74 Monkgate. (House Deeds).
7. Buchanan. T. *William Hayes.*
8. Information supplied by Mr M Powell, 74 Monkgate.
9. Y.R.L. *Kelly's Directories Ltd.* York (1870-1900)
10. Royal Commission. op cit.2. pp 89.90.
11. Information supplied by Mrs C Fairclough, Whitby Drive.
12. Royal Commission. op. cit.2. pp 87-90.
13. Y.C.A. Ac.135. *Bearpark Papers.*
14. Ibid. *Will of Robert Young Bearpark.* 1828.
15. Y.C.A. Peel, B. *The Groves 1860-1881.* In York Historian vol 9.

16. op. cit.13. *Bearpark Papers.*
17. Deed in possession of Mrs G Hall. *Abstract of title of Mr William Chapman to land in Lowther Street.* 1880.
18. Y.C.A. *Council Minutes.* (1850-1851).
19. Y.R.L. *Newspaper Index.*
20. R.C.H. Monuments op. cit.2 pp 90-92.
21. Information supplied by Mr D Poole.
22. Y.R.L. *Newspaper Index.*
23. Y.C.A. York Deeds and Maps.
24. Waterson, E and Meadows, P. *Lost Houses of York and the North Riding.* J Raines. 1990. p 63.

CHAPTER IV
EARLY SCHOOLS

Manchester College

One of the early schools or colleges in this area was Manchester College which was founded in Manchester as a academy for dissenters. (Unitarians etc)in the late 19th century. This school moved to Monkgate in 1803 under the direction of the Rev. Charles Wellbeloved, Minister of the Unitarian church in St. Saviourgate. The college was described in 1819 as a Unitarian Seminary supported by endowments with twenty pupils. It also received annual incomes from charities in Hull, Manchester and Liverpool and £120 a year from Lady Hewley's fund in York.

The work of the college was first carried on in Wellbeloved's house, 38 Monkgate but after 1811 in premises at 33 Monkgate. James Matineau and John Kendrick were two famous pupils at the school in the 1820's. The college finally moved back to Manchester and then to Oxford in 1889. The college premises were bought in 1840 by St. John's College and later used by the Training College for Schoolmistresses.[1]

Archbishop Holgate's Grammar School, Lord Mayor's Walk c.1900. *(Courtesy of Y.R.L.)*

Archbishop Holgate's Grammar School

This School was originally founded in Oglethorpe in 1596 by Archbishop Holgate of York, as a free Grammar School. In the 1850's it was in financial difficulties so in 1858 it amalgamated with the Yeoman School, (which had been built for sons of farmers) which was situated next to St. Johns College on Lord Mayor's Walk. The combined schools, headed by Rev. Robert Daniel, took on the old name of Archbishop Holgate's.

The first years were very hard and the school struggled to keep going. Endowments to the school were sparse and Rev. Daniel and his trustees had difficulty in making ends meet. Books and equipment were in short supply and there was a lack of qualified staff.

The City of York were reluctant to support endowments, however conditions did improve and the school headed by Rev. Johnson and later Mr Percy Vinter, grew in size and reputation. The 1944 Education Act meant that the school was to be largely governed by the City of York, which gave it a sounder financial base.

After the 2nd World War, Brook Street Chapel was purchased and used for classrooms and a gymnasium. A class was also held in an old prefabricated hut, previously used during the war years. The sports fields were on Wiggington Road.

In 1960, a site was purchased on Hull Road, for a new building and the school transferred there in 1961, headed by Mr Donald Frith.[2]

One pupil who attended this school in the 1950's recalled that the building was situated in Lord Mayor's Walk and was the left hand half of what is now all the College of York St. John. It had its own driveway and the frontage is still largely unaltered today. To the extreme left was the headmaster's house, where medical examinations were held. There was also a Boarding House which had about 30 boys of all ages. There was a large school hall which was used for assemblies, and school dinners. At the front of the hall was a platform on which the masters in their gowns sat. One teacher invariably used the same prayer with the indigestible phrase, "And may there never be wanting a succession of persons duly qualified to serve thee in church and state."

Science laboratories, Art and English classrooms occupied the first floor area. The gymnasium with wall bars and a wooden horse was situated in the Brook Street premises. The school playing fields were along Wigginton Road, where the District Hospital is today.

Pupils always addressed each other by their surnames and all the teachers had nicknames. Canings, detentions and a hundred sums were punishments metered out to those who misbehaved. Each "boy" was assigned to a House, Dean, Ebor, Holgate or Johnson. School uniform consisted of a blazer, tie and school cap, which as progression was made towards the sixth form, was pushed further back on the head as a challenge to school authority.[3]

St. John's Training College

The York and Ripon Diocesan Training College for Schoolmasters, later known as St. John's, was established in premises in Monkgate, in 1841, once the home

St. John's College, Lord Mayor's Walk. *(Courtesy of Y.R.L.)*

of Manchester College, as a residential training school. In 1845, a new building was opened in Lord Mayor's Walk at a cost of £11,955. A new practising school which conformed to national standards opened in 1851 in buildings attached to the college. The chapel was built at this time.[4]

Life was hard for these early students, government grants to run the college were meagre and a great deal of time was spent on religious knowledge. The men rose at 5:30am and had to study for one hour, attend religious services and carry out domestic chores before breakfast at 8:00am. Food was sparse, although beer was served with meals. The time honoured way of augmenting the diet was by inter year sporting competitions. The losing year had to provide jam and salmon for the winning team. Until about fifty years ago, sheer financial stringency and a narrow belief that Spartan living and strict seclusion would obtain the best results, seem to have led the college to keep to itself. To be seen by the staff even talking to one of the fairer sex could end the career of a would be teacher. Today the students live a different pattern of life which accords more with the times and many go out to unusual and adventurous posts.[5]

New wings and a gymnasium were all added in the early years of the last century. Teaching and residential accommodation was further increased by annexes in Grays's Court in 1946, Heworth Croft in 1950 and the Limes in 1953. A biology laboratory, library and lecture Hall were all built in the 1950's. There were two hundred and sixty seven students in 1956.

St. John's Secondary Modern School

A Practising School and a Model School of the York and Ripon Diocesan Training College opened in 1851 and 1859 respectively in schoolrooms attached to the College buildings in Lord Mayor's Walk. In 1874 there was eighty-two boys in the Practising School and seventy-nine in the Model School. The schools were complementary, the best teaching methods illustrated in the Model School for students who practised them in the other school. A new combined building was erected close to the site of the college in 1899. From this time the two schools appear to have been considered as one. The school was reorganised in 1932 as a senior boy's school and continued as a voluntary aided secondary modern school in 1948. Two hundred boys were enrolled in 1956.[6]

Mr Elsegood attended this school just after the 2nd World War and enjoyed his time there. He remembered some of the teachers. There was Mr Brennan, the science master who played football for York, Mr McLennan who played rugby and Mr Hobbs, the Headmaster. After school the lads would often play and fight in the moat of the Bar Walls near the school. If caught fighting, they were made to fight it out in the gymnasium.[7]

St. John's Training College for Women

This college was established in 1846 and acquired the building in Monkgate which had been occupied by St. John's College. There were two schoolrooms, one sitting room and twenty bedrooms. There were ten students in 1847 and thirty-seven in 1848. In 1849 there was a staff of two and a visiting teacher for religious instruction. The students were mostly middle class. This college moved to Ripon in the 1860's.[8]

Grey Coat School

This school was established as a charity school in Marygate in 1705 at the same time as the Blue Coat School. It was originally under the control of a Mrs Thornhill but later the administration passed to the "Gentlemen's Committee" who were responsible for the running of the Blue Coat School. This committee handed over the day to day running of the school to a Master and Mistress who were paid a fee for feeding and clothing the girls. This arrangement was often abused, by skimping of food and putting the girls to work for the benefit of the Master and Mistress. Most of the girls were apprenticed into domestic service at varying ages and often placed with farmers in villages near York.

In 1773, William Haughton, an eccentric dancing master, left money to the two charity schools. In 1784, a house originally owned by Luke Farrar, was bought in Monkgate, opposite the County Hospital, for £500, the Marygate property being very run down by this time. Although the new house was altered, conditions there were said to have been cold and spartan. The new house and grounds in Monkgate extended back to the Groves and was originally intended to provide space for the Blue Coat School as well. A high brick wall hid the building from the road. There were spinning and sewing rooms and upstairs a dormitory with eighteen iron bedsteads. Girls slept two in a bed. There was also a kitchen, Matron's apartments and a range of outbuildings. When the Spinning School in St. Andrewgate closed, Mrs Cappe and her Ladie's Committee became involved in the running of the Grey Coat School with "The Gentlemen". They found that many of the girls were diseased and sickly. Some of the past pupils had drifted into prostitution. The Ladies supervised books, clothing and supplies of wool for the spinning school. They also arranged for school visits. This latter system of visits was to continue throughout the life of the school. The cost of maintaining girls in the school in 1786 was £10 a head per annum.[9]

In the years leading up to the 1st World War more leisure activities were provided for the girls. There were trips on the river, a visit to a picture show at the Victoria Hall in Goodramgate and picnics in the country. The girls also attended meetings of the Band of Hope in St. Michael Le Belfrey Church. A punishment book was introduced in 1907 and submitted quarterly to the Gentlemen. Girls were caned for dirty habits. Many were given just bread and water for so many days for running away and insubordination. The last caning took place in 1920. Below is a selection of comments made in the Punishment Book for the early years of the 20th century.

1909.

September. S Holmes, P West, K Neal, B Allen, S Thompson and E Spencer made to stay in. They returned from holiday with dirty heads. S Heathcote to lose a day's holiday for impudence and for bad work in the laundry.

1910.

March. M Boyes to loose $^1/_2$ day holiday for stealing. B Hall the same for rudeness, M Harrison for roughness. E Richardson to be punished for nasty talk.

1911.

May. M Harrison kept away from the Gala to knit her outfit stockings.

1912.

February. A Young and M Harrison had bread and water for two days for insubordination to Miss Crabtree. M Harrison and S Broadbent put on bread and water for running away.

1913.

March. L Thompson to loose $^1/_2$ day holiday for not cleaning out the kitchen flues.

1914.

April. M - caned for drinking water and wetting the bed.

1915.

February. E Clayton was sent on a message but spent the money on sweets then lied and said a soldier had given her the money, caned.

October. E Bradbury locked in the sick room for insolent conduct.

1919.

September. M Paxton, M Bristow and A Hall whipped for depraved habits. L Bailey locked in spare bedroom for insolence and vulgar shouting.

October. All children to loose $^1/_2$ day holiday for bad behaviour. They had taken friends in the garden without permission and cut flowers for them.

November. Girls given one hour scrubbing for untidiness.

1921.

October. G Ibbotson caned for tearing up books and upsetting the ink in school.

November. A Bedford sent to bed for leaving school without permission to post a letter.

December. E Bailey to loose $^1/_2$ day holiday for cutting six inches off her coat when away from the school.[10]

Blanche Martin was only ten when she was sent to the Grey Coat School in the early years of the 20th century having being orphaned at an early age. Her memories of life there weren't very pleasant. She remembered having to scrub the stone step every morning and hit if she didn't scrub hard enough to satisfy the one in charge. Her friend she recalled hated it so much she tried to drink bleach to kill herself. For this she was caned and put on bread and water. Another

Miss Bazzard and Grey Coat Girls in traditional dress. c.1940. *(Courtesy of Y.E.P.)*

friend was crippled most of her life which she blamed on her treatment when young in this Home. Blanche attributed her own bad health in later life to her early years at the Grey Coat School.[11]

Miss Bazzard

In 1921, Miss Gladys Bazzard was appointed Matron at a salary of eighty pounds per annum. In her first few months she replaced the traditional coats with grey coats and had all the girls' hair cut with the resulting fringes seen on photographs of that time. In 1922, a house at Filey, belonging to St. Stephen's Home, was rented for summer holidays. After several years of discussion, schooling for girls and boys was finally combined at St. Anthony's Hall. Girls and boys sat at opposite sides of the classroom. Careers prospects were still restricted for girls, most were still placed in residential domestic service. However the Ladies Committee decided too much time was spent on scrubbing floors and there should be more importance given to school work. The appointment of a new Headmaster at the Blue Coat School was followed by the introduction of organised games for the younger boys and girls, including swimming lessons. They were also taken for more walks and visits to places of interest.

Memories of Grey Coat Girls

Many old Grey Coat girls remembered their days at the school at this time. The day would begin at 6:30 am. Each girl had a job to do before school, such as scrubbing the steps, washing up, dusting etc. In the evenings knitting and mending was done. Bed time was staggered from 6:30pm for the youngest girls, to 9pm for the eldest. Talking was not allowed in the bedrooms. After the closure of the Blue Coat School in 1946, the younger girls attended local elementary schools and the older ones, Burton Stone School for girls, where they were able to mix with other children and enjoy a wider range of activities. They were able to wear the same clothes as other girls. It was decided that the traditional coats and hats should only be worn at the annual service at St. Helen's Church. Some of the old uniforms were given to the York museums. At this time, it was also decided to take in more children, boys and girls from broken homes, because St. Stephen's Home was full.[12]

The Webster Family

Miss Bazzard died in 1959, after thirty eight years of service. She was thought by some of the girls to have been rather strait laced and was not always popular. Her regime was summed up as "Prayers and Cleanliness" and some girls felt that there wasn't much love given to the children in her care. After Miss Bazzard's death, a former Blue Coat old boy, Mr Ernest Webster and his wife agreed to take over the responsibility of the Home until new staff were appointed. The author remembered this time as Mr Webster was her first husband's father. She would take her children to see their grandparents at the school in Monkgate and stay for tea. Her children would play with the other children in the big garden at the back. There was a large climbing frame which was very popular with her family. Although the children, many from broken homes, did not want for material things they lacked the individual love that only parents could give.[13]

Pamela Smith was originally placed at St. Stephen's Home. However in 1959, Mr and Mrs E Webster were asked if Pamela could spend the summer with them at the Grey Coat Schools' annual camp at Filey, as at that time she had no parents to spend the holidays with. They agreed and thus began a deep friendship and relationship with the Webster family that would last for more than forty years.[14]

St. Thomas' Church School

St. Thomas or Groves Church School opened in Cole Street in 1831 in a new building erected by a unknown person. In 1856 it was described as overcrowded and in 1858 the school closed, and the children were transferred to a new building adjacent to St. Thomas's Church in Lowther Street known then as St. Thomas's School. The original school in Cole Street was demolished. The average attendance in 1910 was 356 and fees were still paid. The following are some early extracts from St. Thomas' School log books.[15]

1864.

School in good order but other attainments below average and pupil teachers have done badly in their exams.

St. Thomas' Church School, closed 1957. Demolished 1997.

1865.

School improved, discipline excellent and needlework good but girls careless about their sums.

1869.

Weather very wet. Many girls absent, needed at home.

1870.

Children making lint for wounded soldiers instead of needlework. Home lessons badly done, children punished.

1871.

February. Many children away sick, Scarlet Fever.

July. Children absent because of the York Gala

October. Attendance low owing to severe weather and prevalence of Whooping Cough and measles. More children away. One child died. Two more children have died. One boy returned, absent for more than a year.

November. Attendance low owing to a snow storm, only 44 children at school. Miriam Hornsey could not get to school because of the snow. Had to stop teaching and exercise children to keep them warm.

1872.

January. Willie Dutton playing truant again, found by his mother playing and brought to school.

April. Sent three boys home to get washed.

November. Weather bad. Children had to be exercised indoors. Very dark during last hours of school. Children could not see to work.

Fires would not burn, room filled with smoke.

1879.

June. Many absent because of Scarlet Fever. Many parents would not let their children come to school and the report is that fever is very prevalent in the Groves.

July. Ellen Raisbeck died -fever. John Mortimer died -measles.

1880.

November. A slight inconvenience occurred this morning due to the fact that the keys to the closets were misplaced. Many absent due to measles and illness of mothers.

1881.

March. Epidemic of Scarlet Fever. Emma Glover came in late, playing in playground. As a punishment made to stand on a stool.

December. Two children had spent their school pence.

1882.

February. Two boys drowned in the River Foss.

May. Groves Feast held on the Stray. Mrs Lorriman came to the school and used violent language and took her child away. Child not readmitted until mother apologised.

1883.

January. Did not give my lesson owing to a little misunderstanding with the school cleaner.

E. Mountain and M. Dunford left early to take their father his dinner.

June. Fifth class had a nature lesson in the afternoon instead of the morning because there was only one picture of a camel and the fourth class was using it.

1884.

February. Attendance very poor owing to the bad weather. A urinal should be provided for the boys. E. Carr came in with her lessons imperfectly done. Only one sum done out of four. Excuse given she had a headache.

March. Noticed that the teachers are too fond of leaving their classes to talk to one another especially S Buckley and monitor A. Wakefield.[16]

One ex-pupil of St. Thomas' School remembered that she was only 3 years old when she first went to this school and recalled having to drink horlicks at breaktime, which she has hated ever since. Later, in the junior School, "School milk" was provided, which in the winter months was warmed up by the fire and tasted horrible. She remembered the Headmistress, Miss Leach, and described her as a "bit of a tartar". She recalled the teachers as quite ferocious and remembered one placing her brother, who was talkative, behind a blackboard with sticky tape on his mouth. Other teachers, she recalled, were Miss Evans, who always turned bright red when annoyed, and often wore a dress with square neck and "modesty" vest, and Miss Hornsey who taught the fourth and fifth classes together. She said the standard of teaching was very good and she passed her scholarship and went on to Queen Anne's Grammar School.[17]

Brook Street School

This school opened in 1869 and the York School Board leased these premises until the new Park Grove School was completed in 1895. In 1899 it was reopened to accommodate the lower standards of Park Grove, to relieve the overcrowding in that school. In 1900 there was accommodation for 579 children. Haxby Road School opened in 1904 and then Brook Street became a pupil - teacher centre. From 1906 it was used as a temporary Secondary School for girls. In 1912 it accommodated the boy's department of Shipton Road School. It finally closed in 1915 and the building was sold to Archbishop Holgate's Grammar School in 1944, but was still in use 1957.[18]

St. Wilfrid's School

In the 18th century, a Roman Catholic boy's school known as St. Patrick's was established in Ogleforth and later in a room in the Bedern. The new school St. Wilfrid's was completed in 1875. The site selected was between Monkgate and Groves lane. There was accommodation for three hundred children. The school was divided into three sections. The infants department was on the ground floor. The remaining part was for the upper boys and mixed school. There was ample playground for the children, the girls and infants using one school yard and the boys having their own. They also had their own separate entrances. The entrance for the infants and girls was by way of Groves Lane to Lord Mayor's Walk and the boys had a another entrance down Black Horse passage from Monkgate. Before 1932, a senior girl's department was added. In 1956 there were two schools, a primary school and a secondary girl's school.

In the early days, coal and coke stoves once provided the heating in the classrooms. The children sat in tiers or galleries. The school was very cramped and the children had to use the nearby St. Maurice's Hall as a dining room. This Hall did not have any heating and in winter time the children had to sit in their coats. In Catholic schools the role of the local priest was paramount. In the 1930's, Charles Edward Danson was the school Provost and was held in respect by the pupils and teachers alike. One ex pupil remembered that he rode

St. Wilfrid's Senior Girl's School. 1950.
Back Row: Judith, Pat Hampton, Brenda Appleton, Cath Calpin, Margaret Sempers, Margaret -
Middle Row: Ann Egan, Jean, Anna -, Pat Neale, Mary Grayson
Front Row: Shirley Sims, Maureen Quigley, Pat Binns, Miss Kelly, Sylvia Mizan, Mary Glacken, -, -

a tricycle and had a little Pomeranian dog called Daisy which sat in a basket in front of the bicycle. In his role as school manager he visited the school on a daily basis.

In the early years of the last century, the headmistress was Mother Anthony. Some of the lay teachers were, Miss Alice Gordon, who lived in Park Grove and Miss Nellie Mangan who organised swimming and sports. Other staff were Jenny Bell who lived in Portland Street, Agnes Tate who married Mr Popplewell and Daisy Dixon who lived in St. John Street. A Mr Finney came twice a week to teach P. T. in the schoolyard and he also worked at the library. In the 1920's the children played games on Monk Stray but prior to the Second World War the school made use of the playing fields on Wiggington Road (now the site of the new District Hospital)

The first priority of the school was to teach the pupils to be good Catholics. There was Monday morning checks on who had been to Mass, frequent class visits to church, many visits to the school by the clergy and a lot of religious teachings in the class. There was also a lot of importance laid on passing the scholarship so the pupils could attend St. Michael's in Leeds or the Bar Convent and eventually have good jobs. The prevailing atmosphere throughout the School was one of discipline and strictness and any disobedience would be met by punishment in the form of "strokes of the cane" and a humiliating telling off in front of the class. Sister Denis who was the head in the 1930's was well known for wielding the cane with great vigour and accuracy.[19]

Mrs Pat Calpin, née Ryan, attended St. Wilfrids' School, junior and Senior departments, in the late 1940's and 50's. The Headmistress of the junior school was Sister Celine, and Sister Agnes was head of the senior girls school. Mrs Popplewell, Mr Watson and Miss Galpine, who appeared to be very strict and always rode a bicycle, where just some of the teachers that Mrs Calpin recalled. She also remembered that there was a great emphasis on religious teaching and a strict regime. She was once caned for playing on the Bar walls before school began. When she was in the junior department she was sent by a teacher to buy sweets from a shop in Monkgate. However, as she succumbed to temptation and ate one, she was too frightened to return to school and went home instead.[20]

Mrs Brenda Holmes, née Appleton, attended the senior school in the 1950's. She remembered that Sister Agnes often made them cocoa in school milk bottles, which often broke if the mixture was too hot. Mrs Holmes also recalled that Sister Agnes was enthusiastic and full of energy and quite often entered the classroom hitting her cane against her thigh, ready for action. Religion was always high on the school agenda, often replacing sports activities, if the weather was inclement. Her sister, Audrey, recalled the time she took flowers to school, which she had mischievously picked from a garden in Lumley Road. Unfortunately her actions had been observed and reported to the school. So Audrey was duly punished and the flowers promptly removed from their placement on the altar.

Mrs Holmes' six sisters, Doreen, Audrey, Jean, Eileen, Sheila, Edna and two of her brothers, Bernard and David, all attended St. Wifrid's School between 1940 and 1960.[21]

Park Grove School

Park Grove Board School was opened in 1895 in a new building between Park Grove and Lowther Street. There was accommodation for 1,393 children in two departments, mixed and infants. By 1956 the senior school was for boys only, but there was a junior and infant's school.(22) In the early years of the last century the headmaster was Mr James Olden. The school inspector's report stated that the school at this time was in an excellent state of efficiency, discipline was perfect and the children's education was thoroughly satisfactory. Below is an extract from the school logbooks at this time.

1901.

School closed because of the death of Queen Victoria. Two girls dismissed because an insulting note was brought to the teachers. The piano in the Hall fell over and broke Lily Cass's leg. Students from St. John's College came for teaching practice.

1902.

Lots of sickness. Many children absent because of Measles and Scarlet Fever.

School Inspector's Report: This is an excellent school, teaching very conscientious. One teacher. Miss Matterson of lower standard 1 transferred to Brook Street School because of the unsuitability of the lower hall for teaching purposes. Harry Gibbin drowned whilst playing on the banks of the River Foss, the snow given way. Several children left to attend the new Haxby Road School. 1904- remarkable attendance of one family. Nova, Brian and Denis Shaw have not been absent for eight years. Several boys were troublesome on the way to school. Corporal punishment was administered for disobedience. The photographer, Mr Hayes distributed the annual school prices.

Mr H Hodsman, 34, Lower Eldon Street, who had been a pupil at Park Grove, gained a distinction at Leeds University.

Dr Harold Mann, son of Councillor Mann had attended this school also.

1908.

Many girls absent because of spring cleaning. Mr James Olden retired.

1910.

School closed owing to funeral of late King. Florence Gibbs won a "Dorothy Wilson" Scholarship. School visit to Wombwell's Menagerie. Empire Day, half day holiday.

Outbreak of fire in St. VI girl's room during an experiment. Miss Carr burnt her foot.

1913.

Ramble down Tang Hall Lane. Eleven classes taught on first floor, five on the ground floor. One class taught in the central hall. The practice of teaching two classes in one room discontinued.

1914.

A fund for Belgian Refugees started. Three large mufflers, four helmets, eighteen pairs of socks and forty pairs of mittens sent to Lady Helmsley for soldiers. 59 Union Terrace furnished by the staff and children for Belgian Refugees. Boys of the Manor School accommodated in Park Grove, requisition of the Military of their school. Shared the school with Haxby Road. One week Parkgrove mornings, next week afternoons.

1916.

Reopened school at Park Grove.

May.

Low attendance due to Zeppelin raid.

June. Little boy killed by car, Mrs Neale's son.

September. Reginald Oakley, second year student at St. John's, formerly pupil teacher at Groves School, killed in France. Further supply of socks knitted for military. Zeppelin raid affected attendance.

1917.

January. Bitterly cold, problem with the heating.

February. James Farrell drowned in Foss. Donald Wilkinson had a lucky escape. March. School closed for a week to remove stock and furniture to temporary premises to be used during Military Occupation of school. Boys to go to Centenary Chapel St. Saviourgate, girls to Brook Street school and infants to Methodist Chapel, Monkgate.

April. Snow, 12 ins of snow and a blizzard blowing. Captain Bert Bryant, a former pupil and pupil teacher of the school killed in France. War economy lectures held. Invitations to mothers. Lessons in war savings and economy in food to pupils in top class.

1918.

Boys collected waste paper and $^1/_2$ ton chestnuts for use in munitions factory. Tank in Market Street also airship and aeroplane, low attendance. Brother of teacher, Mrs Robinson killed.

July. Low attendance due to Influenza outbreak. Many departments in the city closed. July 4th. American Independence Day. Celebrations and hospitality given to American troops in the city.

October. Many boys absent, potato picking. School closed for two weeks- Influenza outbreak.

November. 11th. Armistice signed. Top Boys. Harry Quinn, Albert Baxter, Les Farmery, G Lofthouse, Mark Wells, Robert Kirk, Les Barker, Geo. Kilham, Harry Scaife, H. Barker and W Readman.[23]

Chapter IV. Notes and References.
1. V.C.H. p.456.
2. A.H.G.S. *The first Four Hundred and Fifty Years.* (1996) Smith, Easingwold.
3. Information supplied by former pupil.
4. Op. Cit. 1. P.452-3
5. Y.R.L. *The Story of St. John's College.* In Dalesman (1976).
6. V.C.H. p.452.
7. Information supplied by Mr B Elsegood, Moatfield, Osbaldwick.
8. V.C.H. p.452.
9. Taylor, W. *History of the Blue and Grey Coat Schools.* (1995).
10. Borthwick. *Grey Coat School Punishment Book.* YCT/GCS No/3.
11. Information supplied by Mrs Jean White, Badger Hill.
12. Memories of former Grey Coat Girls.
13. Memories of the Author (Mrs A Appleton, formerly Webster)
14. Information supplied by Mrs Pamela Smith, Dijon Avenue.
15. V.C.H. p.455.
16. Y.C.A. *St. Thomas' School log books* (1850-1880).
17. Memories of a former pupil and ex. Groves resident.
18. V.C.H. p.455.
19. Lee and Cuthbert. *Without a City Wall.* History of St. Wilfrid's R.C. School. (1995) Maxiprint. Pp.17 39-42.
20. Information supplied by Mrs P Calpin, née Ryan.
21. Memories of Mrs B Holmes, née Appleton, and Mrs A Goodman, née Appleton.
22. V.C.H. p.450.
23. Y.C.A. *Park Grove log books* (1900-1919).

Aerial view of Park Grove School wth part of Huntington Road and Lowther Street. c.1900.

CHAPTER V
TO CHURCH OR CHAPEL

St. Thomas' Church

St. Thomas' Church was opened in 1854 at the far end of Lowther Street to cater for the spiritual needs of a fast expanding population in the Groves area. The nearest church before this time was St. Maurice, situated on the corner of Monkgate and Lord Mayor's Walk.

St. Thomas' Church Choir. c.1950 *(Courtesy of D Sturdy)*

Church Minutes

Below are some abstracts from the church minutes in the 1920' and 30's.
1925.
Death of Mr G Allitt. Resignation of Rev. J C Walker. St. Thomas's Bazaar to be held. Scout's sub committee to meet Parent's committee regarding erection of a scout hut. The Garden Party to be held in the vicarage gardens on Haxby Road. Annual choir outing. Mrs Sherwood and Mrs Barrett to arrange a play or pageant. Tea, concert and dance to be held in the Grand. Sunday collection for the County Hospital. Mr Sadler in charge of the choir. Mr and Mrs Ham to be caretakers. Miss Gibson to arrange a concert. Ladies sewing party. Mr Wilson to be a member of the choir.

1st St. Thomas' Scouts. Outside the church. Geoffrey Morton far right, middle row. c. 1920 *(Courtesy of Mrs G. Hall)*

13th York St. Thomas' Guides. Outing to North East Coast. 1936.
(Courtesy of Mrs Yorke)

Park Grove (1890s) Infants. *(Courtesy of Mr N. Acomb)*

Park Grove (1920s) Girls. *(Courtesy of Mrs G. Hall)*

Park Grove Girls with Athletics Shield. c.1925 *(Courtesy of Mrs G. Hall)*

St. Thomas' School (1930s) *(Courtesy of Mrs N. Mooring)*

A cricket match to be held the day after the garden fete. Mr Shepherd, Mr Vasey and Mr Harding to organise. Twenty four Brownies in pack. Brownie Revels joined by Groves. J Watson to be organist and choir master. G. F. S. Rally in Hull. Carol Heavsides and Susan Lambert to be leaders. Twenty children in the Kindergarten. Mrs Vera Thompson to play the piano for Sunday School.

1939.

Vicar, Rev. Lloyd Mc Dermitt. Assistant curate, Rev. Penniston.

Lay Reader, Mr Bell, Chestnut Avenue. Church wardens, F. Davies, Park Grove. C. Sutton, Feversham Crescent. Synodsmen. D. Allit. A. Atkinson, H. Davies, Dodsworth A. Douglas, H. Huffenden, Jackson, Lane, Mathews, Murphy and J. Shepherd. Organist and choir master, Mr J Wilson. Heworth Green. Sextoness, Mrs Ward, Lowther Street. Clothing Club, Monday, Parish room.

Other families involved with the church at this time were the Hodsman, Sutton, Temple, Thompson and Lane families. Mrs Laverack of Neville House, Mrs Bell of Haxby Road and Mrs Belt of Clarence Street were just some of the ladies also mentioned in the church minutes.

1965.

A legacy from the late Miss Grace Darley received.

1967.

The Rev. R. M. Firth to be the new Vicar of St. Thomas. St. Maurice's parish to be amalgamated to St. Thomas. Two bells, the altar from the Lady Chapel and other furnishings from St. Maurice received. St. Thomas Mother's Union, Fifty three members. Girl Guides to clean church silver for Advent, G.F.S. for lent. Mrs Brydon and Mrs Cox to change and wash altar linen. Mrs Shepherd to wash choir boy's ruffles[1]

Guides and Brownies

In 1921, Miss Bertha Peters who was in charge of the young lady's bible class held in the parish room every Sunday afternoon and the sewing class every Monday evening decided to form a Guide company in St. Thomas' parish. Miss Sherlock, the Commissioner for Guides came to talk to interested parties about the purpose and aims of the Guide movement. A Guide company. the 13th York St. Thomas was eventually formed with Miss Mockett as the first Captain and a handful of enthusiastic members. A Brownie pack was also formed at this time. In 1981 the Company celebrated its Diamond Jubilee when Margaret Ward was the Captain.[2]

St. Maurice's Church

A new church dedicated to St. Maurice was completed in 1878 at a cost of £7,083. the architect was Charles Fisher of York. It stood on the site of the old church and comprised a nave with north and south aisles, a chancel and a square

St. Maurice's Church, demolished 1967

tower with four bells, two of which probably came from the former church.[3] This church flourished in the first half of the last century, with full congregations, even though it had to compete with St. Thomas and two Methodist Chapels. There were Sunday Schools bible classes, mother's union and a girls club. Guides, Brownies, Scout and Cub packs were formed during the 1920's and 1930's and a youth club during the 1940's. The Scout hut was in the garden of the rectory, at 38 Monkgate.[4]

Mrs Amy Morton remembered attending the girl's club at St. Maurice in the 1930's, run by a Miss Ingham. She also recalled attending church services every Sunday during lent, in order to collect religious stamps for her album. Mrs Morton also remembered a lady called "Blind Mary", who lived in a cottage on the corner of Groves Lane, and who sat at the front of the church, in straw hat, apron and bib, with a large Braille hymn book, singing loudly, and often out of tune. Mrs Morton also belonged to St. Maurice Girl's Club, and once a year they held a social evening to entertain the girls from the Grey Coat School. The Grey Coat girls all wore grey dresses with white collars and white bonnets for church, she recalled.[5]

In the 1940's and 50's the Rector was the Rev. Bulmer and there was a very good choir who enjoyed many outings. The organist, in the late 1930's was Ted

Prangnell, who was the music teacher at Mill Mount and Nunthorpe Schools. Later there was a Mr Smith, Mr Grant and Mr Neville Scott.

Mr Michael Mead was a member of the choir in the 1940's. He recalled that an annual service was always held in Holy Trinity Church, Goodramgate, which was joined with St. Maurice. He remembered that, choir members had to push the piano from St. Maurice to Holy Trinity in order to provide the music accompaniment.

The Bradford, Brown, Burrell, Burton, Guest, Lane, Mead, Moiser, Poole, Ripley and Smith, were just some of the families involved with the choir and church at this time.[6]

In the 1960's congregations became smaller, due to the demolition of many of the houses in the Groves area. In 1967, it was decided to demolish this church, in order to widen the corner of Monkgate and Lord Mayor's Walk, for York's inner ring road scheme. The last service was held on Sunday August 21st 1967 and the Rector was Rev. Gaunt. Church members were offered the memorial plates and the organ was given to St. John's College. The new Church, in Acomb, St. James the Deacon, received the Norman arch, two bells and four stained glass windows. Two bells, the altar, from the Lady Chapel, and other furnishings were sent to St. Thomas' Church.[7]

St. Maurice's Choir outing. c.1950. *(Courtesy of Mr M Mead)*

Groves Methodist Chapel

By the 1860's, the Groves area was beginning to be built up. It contained a population of just over 5,000, or about one eighth of the whole of the citizens of York. Outside the city walls between Bootham and Hull Road there were only two places of worship, St. Maurice and St. Thomas(1853). Such were the conditions in York when a small group of Wesleyans decided that there was a need for more spiritual work in the Groves area. The first meeting was held in a room over a stable at the end of Brownlow Street and was approached by a wide passage. Their numbers steadily increased and it was decided that bigger premises were needed.

Brook Street Chapel

Eventually a piece of land was acquired in Brook Street, near Pilgrim Street and Cole Street, on which to erect a Wesleyan School Chapel. From Mondays to Fridays the building was to be used as a day school and on Sundays as a place of worship. In March 1868, the building, comprising a large hall, vestries and classrooms was opened and dedicated by the President of the Conference, the Rev. J Bedford. The results that followed the opening of the building more than justified all the hard work. The day school was attended by six hundred scholars. The headmaster was Mr J Olden and Miss Jane Pipes was in charge of the infant's department. More than four hundred children attended the Sunday School. The services on a Sunday were crowded and the membership of Brook Street rose steadily in the next twenty years.

The New Chapel

In 1882, there was still only one nonconformist place of worship in this large area outside the city walls and a decision was made to build a new chapel in the Groves. A site in Cotford Place in Clarence Street, was purchased at cost of £1, 300 and on the 12th of September the foundation stones were laid. The first stone was laid by Mr William Leak and other stones by Mrs Edward Hoyle and the City Sheriff, Coun. J Sykes Rymer. This chapel opened in 1884 but the Brook Street premises continued to be used as a Sunday School and Day School. The formation of the School Board in 1889 brought a change in the educational system of the city and when the Park Grove Elementary School was opened in 1890, the children were transferred there from Brook Street.

All the zeal and fervour of the early Methodists were present in the Groves society in those days. The congregations were very large and there were many class meetings, missions and teas. Before the introduction of the National Insurance scheme, the members of the Chapel were looking after the material as well as the spiritual welfare of their neighbours. Grants from the Poor Fund were regularly paid to needy widows and those experiencing hard times. It is impossible to record here all those who worked tirelessly for the chapel in those early days but four names will always be associated with the Sunday School, Mr Benjamin Wales, Mr John Brown, Mr Thomas Thurgood, and Mr Edward Hill, the chapel's first organist and a class leader. Four men who have been associated with the work at the Groves chapel have also served on the York City Council. Alderman Joseph Agar and Alderman R Vernon Wragge were both Lord Mayor three times, Alderman C T Hutchinson, an old Groves Sunday School scholar was Lord Mayor in 1937-1938 and Alderman William Thompson held the position of chief magistrate in 1943-44.

The faithful work of the people at Groves continued throughout the early years of the 20th century. Missions were held and were often accompanied by midnight marches when members would assemble in the city and headed by the Groves Mission Band would march to the chapel for a midnight meeting. This band under its conductor Mr A Lickley, would lead Sunday School scholars to the station when they went on their annual trip to the seaside as well as heading numerous parades and processions. It finally became merged into the Rowntree's Cocoa Works Band in 1903.

Groves Chapel, closed in the 1970's. *(Courtesy of Y.R.L.)*

During the 1st World War the rooms at the back of the chapel were taken over by the Military and alternative accommodation had to be found for the class meetings. In spite of this the services were fully attended and much good work continued. In 1920 a memorial tablet to the 17 men associated with the Groves area was unveiled and dedicated in the vestibule by the Rev. C Annis. The years following the war were some of the most difficult in the chapel's history. In common with other Christian denominations, the Groves chapel during the inter war years, was faced with declining congregations. In an age when scientific developments were providing more material advantages, the community seemed not to need the comfort that was previously acquired from their faith.[8] It may be that the decline in numbers attending church had been commented upon earlier, but then the reason given was blamed on the preachers. Someone writing in the York Methodist Monthly in 1898, wrote, "If preachers would cease from flirting with butterfly beauties at garden parties, attending theatres and music halls and give more time to prayer, visiting the sick, caring for the poor and make the market place their pulpit occasionally, they would not lack hearers on a Sunday" One wonders if this reader had one particular preacher in mind when he wrote this.[9] However the good work by the people at the Groves went on during the inter war years. A choir of more than 200 boys and girls, trained by Mr Robert Dunwell, sang at the Anniversary services. Music and singing had always played an important part in the worship at the Groves and under the conductorship of Mr Dunwell, the musical concerts brought packed audiences. The Mother's Meetings flourished at this time too due to the work of Mrs Wilkinson, Mrs Kendrew, Mrs Wain and Mrs James Bowman.

The 2nd World War brought fresh difficulties and once again the chapel was taken over by the Military. In the autumn of 1940, a canteen was opened for service men and every night for nearly five years a hot meal was provided. Although the chapel escaped damage on the night of 28th April, 1942, bombs fell less than 400 yards away. Many young men and women associated with the chapel served in His Majesty's Forces at home and overseas. It was during the war years that it became apparent that the Brook Street premises were a financial liability and the trustees felt compelled to sell. The building was sold to the Governors of Archbishops Holgate's Grammar School in 1945 for £4,500.

After the war years there was no sign of any increase in the size of the Sunday congregations but the loyalty and enthusiasm of the members was still evident. In 1946 it was announced that a London company of promoters was seeking permission to establish a dog racing track on the Rugby ground in Wigginton Road. The Minister of the Groves Chapel, supported by Anglicans, the schools and hospital authorities in the area organised a petition, which was submitted to York City Council. The promoters finally decided not to proceed with their application. In the 1950's and 60's most of the housing that lay between Lord Mayor's Walk and Lowther Street was demolished and Groves Chapel finally closed for services in the 1970's.[10]

Monkgate Methodist Chapel

The Primitive Methodists built this Chapel in Monkgate and it was opened in 1903. It was also known as the John Petty Memorial Chapel as it was dedicated to the memory of John Petty, first governor of Elmfield College and was built with special seating accommodation for the students from this College. The building cost over £8,000 including fittings.[11]

Archie Sargent

In the 1930's, the life of Monkgate Chapel was enhanced by the arrival of Archibald William Sargent as choir master. He was born in 1897 in Sittenbourne, in Kent, into a staunch Primitive Methodist family. His parents were musical and even at an early age Archie showed signs of his musical abilities. After the war he entered the Civil Service and in 1921 two great ambitions were realised. He married Janet Heywood, who shared his love of music, and had a fine mezzo-soprano voice and was also a talented pianist. He was also posted to the office of the Inland Revenue in York, a town that was well known for its choral singing. In 1930, after a spell of looking after the choir of Victoria Bar Chapel, Archie was asked to take on both the choir and organ at Monkgate Chapel by Walton Batley, music master at the associated Elmfield College. So began twenty-one momentous years of his life. During the dark days of the 2nd World War when active choirs were few, the name Monkgate became an inspiration to many weary and depressed people in many parts of the world. Choir membership rose steadily from 15 in 1930 to a peak of 105 in 1945/46. In the war years, with all the hazards and stresses of war, conscription, fire service and air raids the loyalty and effort given by the choir members was phenomenal. As well as the Sunday services the choir gave concerts at Cawood, Malton and Pocklington, There were the Ebor Day services in the Minster, carol services, visits to local hospitals and overcrowded performances of the Messiah to name just a few of the annual events. But what brought the choir its most widespread fame, was the series of twenty two BBC radio broadcasts, mainly hymn recitals, between 1937 and 1947. This produced a massive post bag from many parts of the country and even some from countries as far away as Italy, Libya, South Africa and the U S A. It was at this time too, that The Sargent Singers, a highly flexible and mobile mini-choir was formed to respond at short notice to urgent requests for concerts. Sometimes as many as eleven out of fourteen evenings involved choir activities. Through all these years Archie Sargent was faithfully supported by his wife Janet. He attributed the success of the choir to the enthusiasm and loyalty of the members, his wife's support and the fact that he always started rehearsals with a prayer. However, in 1951, having realised that the choir had passed its zenith he resigned. He later joined the Methodists at Clifton, after a spell at the Priory Street Chapel. He died in 1973 and his wife fifteen years later. So ended a remarkable chapter in the history of amateur music making in York and Yorkshire created by two people with a love of music and love of the city.[12]

Memories of Choir Members

Archie Sargent's son, Brian Sargent, remembered some of the choir and chapel members from these days. In the mid 1930's, the Minister was the dearly loved, Walter Scott Bosence. He made a great hit with the listening public when he compered the Monkgate choir's first broadcast in 1937. However he was forced to return back to Cornwall where he had been born, because of his wife's ill health.

Amos Watson, the Monkgate choir's senior tenor, unmistakable with a bald head and impressive paunch had a calming influence on any moments of heated debates in the choir's A.G.M. He and his wife Edith, a contralto in the choir, farmed Fourth Mile Stone farm along Malton Road. Mr Sargent as a school boy had spent many a happy afternoon at this farm, playing on a derelict lorry. Just before the 2nd World War, the Watsons retired from the farm and moved to 75 Monkgate, a dignified three storey terrace house, near Monkgate roundabout. Another valued member of the choir at this time was G.E. (Ted) Jackson, who had a rich bass voice. At the performance of Harold Moore's expressive Lent Contata "The Darkest Hour" by the combined Monkgate and Baptist choirs at Priory Street Baptist Church in 1945, Ted sang the demanding role as Christ with great credit. He was also a member of the 17 strong mini choir, The Sargent Singers, formed in March 1940, to respond to needs which larger choirs could not meet. He was also one of a group of singers recruited to visit Church Fenton on 28 December 1945 in response to a desperate appeal by the B.B.C. who were to transmit a Young Farmer's Xmas party with sixty people too shy to sing. In the 1960's, Mr Jackson joined Heworth Chapel and helped to form a junior choir. Another choir member Mr Sargent remembered was Olive Laverick, solo soprano and elegant wife of Percy Laverick, the gentle and kindly pharmacist of 85 Clarence Street. He remembered that she was totally desolate after her husband's sudden death in 1951. Ron Smith who ran a small one man garage and engineering workshop in Monkgate near St. Maurice's Church was another member of the chapel and family friend. He was a very genial man and once agreed to mend Mr Sargent's old 1938 James/villiers two stroke motor bike, which Mr Sargent had acquired second hand, but had no knowledge of its mechanical workings. Mr Sargeant also recalled, Evelyne Smith who in the 1940's attended the Chapel with him to provide the piano accompaniment for the Junior Christian Endeavour meetings. The Spavin family, from St. John's Street, the Cockrill family from Neville Street and the Nash family from Park Grove, where just some of the families involved with the Chapel at this time. Mr Sargent also recalled that on evenings near Christmas from at least 1937 to 1950 inclusive, the Monkgate Choir would go to the Workhouse or The Grange as it was later called, to sing carols. After which they moved on to St. Hilda's Children's Home. These visits were also made at Harvest Festival time.[13]

Chapter V. Notes and References.
1. Borthwick. Y/St. Thomas' *Church Minutes.* (1931-1967).
2. Information supplied by Miss Yorke, Danebury Drive, Acomb.
3. V.C.H. p.395.
4. Information supplied by Mr M Mead, Fulford.
5. Memories of Mrs Amy Morton, Heworth.
6. Information supplied by Mr M Mead.
7. Y.E.P. September 1967.
8. Gardener, W B. *The Unfinished Story.* (1949) Coultas and Volans.
9. Y.R.L. York Methodist Messenger. *History of our Methodist Chapels.*
10. Op. cit. 8. Gardener.
11. V.C.H. p.415.
12. Sargent, B. *A Thousand Tongues.* In Dalesman. (September 1993).
13. Information supplied by Mr B Sargent, Norwich.

CHAPTER VI

LIFE IN THE 1920s AND 1930s

Mrs Webster's Memories

Mrs Rose Webster grew up in Lowther Street in the 1920's. Her mother had died when she was young so she was brought up by her Aunt and uncle, Mr and Mrs "Ossie" Garrett who owned a greengrocer's shop in Lowther Street. Her granny, Mrs Annie Smith, had lived in Lower Eldon Street. In those days there was Lower, Middle and Upper Eldon Street. Now Upper Eldon Street is called Del Pyke. There was a church called Del Pyke in Oglethorpe, demolished in the 16th century. Mrs Webster remembered some of the shops and shopkeepers from her youth. There was Lovely's fish shop, fish 2d, chips 1d, Atkinson's hardware shop, which sold paraffin and soldered pans and Slater's chemist where you could buy a remedy for any ailment for just pennies. At Jimmy Benson's bike shop, a Raleigh roadster could be hired for a penny a week. There were only a few cars on the roads then but bicycles were very popular and a status symbol. At dinner and home time it was impossible to cross the Haxby Road because of Rowntree's workers on their bicycles. Mrs Webster also recalled the horse drawn carts that frequently came round the Groves. There was the man who sold herrings, 12 for a shilling, the coal man who rang a little bell, selling coal at two and six, and the rag and bone men who gave goldfish for payment for rags. There was also the shops were you could get a $1/_2$d on a jam jar and 4d on a undamaged rabbit skin. Nearly everyone shopped at the Co-op and looked forward to collecting their "Divvy". In the summer months she played with other children in the streets. Skipping ropes, whips and tops, battledores and shuttle cocks were popular with the girls. She also recalled playing hopscotch, tiggy and marbles. Books could be bought from paper shops for $1/_2$d, usually second hand. There was always entertainment in the streets with the Salvation Army band, Burlington Bertie and the organ grinder and his monkey. Once a man came round the streets with a dancing bear. She attended St. Wilfrid's school, which she enjoyed very much. Because she was one of the top pupils, she was selected to take French. She remembered the school trips on the "River King" and eating Barton's buns. On her way to school she had to pass the Industrial school in Lowther Street, which was a school for wayward girls. There was a bell outside this school which children would often pull and then run away. Once when there was a fire at the school the girls had to vacate the building by the fire escape and she recalled them all sitting on the steps singing. When she was older Mrs Webster would go with a friend to the Grand cinema in Clarence Street. It was a cinema and dance hall combined. It would cost $2^1/_2$d to see Tom Mix.[1]

Memories of Park Grove School

Amy Morton, née Bond, was born in 1913 at her father's shop in Brownlow Street. She started Park Grove School on 22nd May 1918 when the Headmaster was Mr Prince. Her sister Clara, a year older than her, would not go to school on her own so they both started together. During the 1st World War, this school was used for military purposes, so she and her sister went to the Methodist Chapel in Monkgate. One of her earliest memories was leaving her home in Fern Street and then going into Lockwood Street and down the ally next to the chapel. This chapel had railings round it and she remembered that her mother would pass food to them through the railings at break time. Her brother Charles, born 1915 and known as "Sonnie" started school in August 1918. Once he came home with the wrong cap and all three children caught ringworm from this incident. Their heads had to be shaved and they were all absent from school for a year. Her mother made them mop caps to wear. She remembered that the headmistress of the infant school was Mrs Askam and Miss Rispin and Miss Hopkins were two of the teachers then. When she was older she was made a flower monitor, but she remembered that the water always smelt, as it was only changed once a week. At eleven she helped the school win an athletic's trophy against other schools in York. She chose a clock for winning the sack race and received an orange candle stick for being in the winning rally team. Mrs Waind was the headmistress of the senior girls and other teachers were Miss Watson, Miss Ingham and Miss Batty. Miss Ingham, she recalled, lived in St. John's Street

Benson's Bike Shop in Lowther Street. *(Courtesy of Y.C.A.)*

and ran St. Maurice's Girl's Club with Miss Sykes. There was also a teacher called Mr Coupland. He had been a conscientious objector in the 1st World War and his nickname was "Conshy Coupland" The caretaker was a Mrs Clarke who lived in Princess Street. For a month before she left school, Mrs Morton went to the White Cross Lodge along Haxby Road to learn housewifery skills. She was taught every thing about caring for a home, baking, dusting and washing. There was also a doll called Archibald and all the pupils had to learn to look after it. When she was at school, boys and girls were taught separately but in the 1930's they were mixed classes. Her sister Audrey, who started school in 1931 won a thimble for sewing and a china cup and saucer for good work.

Charles Harold Bond, brother of Amy, was born in 1915. He recalled his days at Park Grove School. A Mr Smith taught history and cricket when he attended this school. If the cricket team played on a Saturday and lost, all the team were caned on the following Monday, so they had all the weekend to think about it. Mr Smith sometimes placed a 3d or 6d piece on the cricket bails and if anyone bowled him out they could have the money. Mr Bond did not remember him giving much money away. He remembered some more of the teachers. There was a Mr Hawkins, he was a tall thin man who taught geography and lived in Lowther Street. A Mr Coupland, science and maths and a Mr Coates who was noted for his excessive use of the cane. The latter was found dead on Strensall Common in 1927.

Bond Family outside their shop. c.1898.
This shop received a direct hit by a bomb in January 1941. *(Courtesy of Y.C.A.)*

Park Grove Rounder's Team. c.1940. Audrey Bond 1st on left, back row.
(Courtesy of Mrs G Hall)

Mrs Morton's Memories

Mrs Amy Morton remembered her Aunt and Uncle, Joseph and Winifred Bond who had a grocer's shop, 1 Waverley Street in the 1930's. Her uncle had several motor bikes. One had a sidecar made from basket ware and crowds would watch him on a Sunday morning attach the sidecar to the bike. They would always go for a ride every Sunday (No Sunday opening then).

She also recalled some more of the shopkeepers living in the Groves in the 1930's. There was a Mr lobley who was an undertaker. He lived at 16 Brownlow Street and next door was a yard with a workshop above where he made the coffins. You can still see the workshop today Mrs Morton added. Mr Millard had a newsagent's shop in Garden Street, near the back entrance to St. John's College. One of his arms was only a stump, possibly as a result of serving in the 1st World War. He would fold the papers and tuck them under his stump. At the corner of March Street was a butcher's shop, Ridsdale. Robin Lake was an apprentice and she recalled him delivering meat on a bike with a basket on the front. He still delivered her meat to her when she moved to Heworth. Eventually Mr Lake took over the running of the butcher's shop and still has a butcher's in Lowther Street today. Granny Watson had a greengrocer's shop at 31 Brownlow Street which had a long garden with fruit trees. She always ordered a small loaf from Mrs Morton's parent's shop, Bond's. As a girl, Mrs Morton would take the bread to Granny Watson's shop and received a pear an apple or plum from a drawer under the counter. In the 1950's, a Mr Barber moved in here and the shop changed to a barber's. Mr and Mrs Hudson lived opposite at 34 Brownlow Street and Blackburn, Stansfield, Stobbard, Howden, Kelly and McJannett were just some more families that lived in that street then. She also remembered the Atkinson, Creaser, Gott, Lea and Quinn families that lived in Dudley Street. Mr Atkinson was a tin smith and had a pot and pan shop in Lowther Street. When she was a girl she lived in Fern Street, and she remembered during the 1st World War that the gas mantles would go dim when a zeppelin raid was imminent. Her mother would put her and her sister and brother in a cupboard under the stairs during the raid. When their Grandfather died in 1924, Amy and her sister Clara had to have black dresses. A dressmaker, Miss Ibbetson, who lived in Fern Street made them in black and white check material so they could wear them afterwards and they wouldn't look so severe.

In Eldon Street in the 1920's and 30's there were many small shops and people who worked from home. In Eldon Street there was Field's off licence, Swan's dairy, Hodsman's joiners and undertakers and a sweet shop run by a Mr James. In the same street, Mr Morley was a cobbler and old Mrs Morley did the heavy washing for other people in her own home. In the 1930's there was a post office in Neville Street and Mr Piercy sold groceries and sweets from a shop next to the church hall in this same street. The Questa family lived in Townend Street and they pushed a cart through the streets selling ice cream. They also had a shop in King's Square, on the corner of St. Andrewgate and a stall on the market. Mr Slater was a druggist in Townend Street and Mrs Morton remembered that her sister Audrey once scalded her arm and he bandaged it up for her. He wasn't qualified so he couldn't call himself a pharmacist, but people living in the Groves would always go to him to buy something for their ailments. Kidd's shoe repairers had a shop in Townend Street also. Horners had the fish shop and Crowes was a wholesale grocers. In the 1950's there was a second hand tool shop near the end of Little Silver Street called Reeves Mrs Morton remembered. Hutchinson's post office and grocer's shop was at the corner of Townend Street and Clarence Street. Next door to Hutchinson's in Townend Street was Crowe's butchers who sold meat and pork pies. In Walpole Street, Pickards had the fish shop and there was a butcher's shop down that street also. There was a Co-op at the Haxby Road end of Vyner Street and a "Tea Time" shop on Haxby Road.

Mrs Morton remembered some of the shops that were in Monkgate and Lord Mayor's Walk when she was a girl. Prior to the second World War, Bowman's Removals had their premises on the chapel side of Monkgate. After the war Harold Smith's Auto Parts took over the premises. Binns sold tyres for cars and Leckonby had a sweet shop in Monkgate. Mr West had his building works near Monk Bridge roundabout and Mr Rymer the coal merchant was on the opposite side of the road, near Foss Bank. Wrightson's fruit shop was on the corner of Lord Mayor's Walk and Goodramgate, where Bulmer's shop is now, they used a horse and cart to deliver and sell the fruit around the streets, she recalled. George Elsegood had his bicycle shop on Lord Mayor's Walk where now is Bob Trotter's. There was a chemist, Medley's, where the Doll's shop is now and also a shop that sold second hand collars.

In the 1930's Mr Atkinson had his iron monger's shop in Penley Grove Street. At the side of that shop was an alley were there was a bakery. The baker Mr Gray supplied all the shops in the area. He later emigrated to Australia and Les Grant took over the bakery. Les Grant then moved to Lowther street and had a cake shop and bakery there. His wife had a draper's shop next door. There were two branches of the Lane family, one lived at no 8 Dudley Street and one lived in Lowther Street. They were both coal merchants but the family from Lowther Street also had a shop selling groceries and sweets, Benson's bike shop was in Lowther Street in the 1920's to 50s and Mr Phillips had his hairdresser's business next door. There were two fish shops not far away from each other. Hepworth's was on the corner of Princess Street and Lowther Street and Alliance or Eldon Street Fisheries further up.[2]

Frank Fowler, Boxer in the 1920's. *(Courtesy of Mr R Fowler)*

The Fowler Family

Mr Richard Fowler's parents grew up in the Groves area in the 1920' and 1930's. His grandfather, Mr Arthur Fowler had lived in Union Terrace a street just off Clarence Street. When Mr Arthur Fowler was 16, he signed up for the army and was sent to South Africa to fight in the Boer War. He was wounded in the first months he was there and was sent home on a hospital ship. Although he lost a lung Mr Fowler lived until he was eighty-four. Mr Fowler was a master builder and built some of the houses in Markam Street. In the course of his building work he often found Roman remains which he presented to the Yorkshire Museum and was made an honorary Member of the Yorkshire Philosophical Society. He often did contract work for the City Council and once, chasing up an overdue account, presented himself at the Mansion House when there was a civic function. He was immediately reimbursed. During the first years of the last century when there wasn't much building work to be had in the York area he went to work in Canada. He took some men with him from the Groves and they helped to build McGill University, Montreal in Quebec. He also took his family with him. One son was born on the St. Lawrence Seaway and was subsequently named Lawrence. Because Mr Fowler spent so many years working in Canada he acquired a Canadian accent and when he returned to the Groves he was known as "Canada Fowler".

Mr Richard Fowler's father, Mr Frank Fowler, left school at eleven or twelve and went to work on the land. Because he was tall for his age and it was during the 1st World War he managed to escape the notice of the school inspectors. When he was only seven he worked as a callboy at the Theatre Royal earning 2/6d a week. When he was older he was apprenticed to a butcher in Gillygate. One of his tasks was to kill a pig. As he was inexperienced he did not do the job properly and the unfortunate animal managed to escape but still had the cleaver stuck in its neck. It ran squealing down Gillygate and another butcher had to finish off the job and put the poor animal out of its misery. When he was a young man, Mr Frank Fowler excelled at all sports, but in the 1920's became a professional boxer. He attributed his prowess at boxing to the fact that he was once set on in the Groves by a rival gang from the Walmgate area. He obtained his revenge by tackling each one as they left work. He also took part in blind boxing matches at the York Gala. He did a lot of his training at the back of the Exhibition pub at the corner of Bootham and Gillygate. He fought as a light heavy weight and held the record for beating most champions of other countries in the 1920's. He also fought and won Max Schmelling, who had previously fought against Joe Lewis. Mr Fowler featured on cigarette cards of the age.

The Lovely Family

In 1928. Mr Frank Fowler married Elsie Lovely. Her family had owned the fish shop in Penley Grove Street, at the corner of March Street, since the early years of the 20th century. Elsie and her sister Nessie attended St. Wilfrid's school and both excelled at sports. Elsie was a good swimmer and often dived off Lendal Bridge. She also won many swimming championships and swam against men and won. As a young woman, Elsie was keen on riding motorbikes and once went through the window of a Chinese restaurant in Gillygate on a machine loaned from Syd Haw, who owned a garage at the end of Lowther Street. Elsie

The Lovely Family, outside the fish shop. c.1920. *(Courtesy of Mr R Fowler)*

was also an accomplished piano and piano accordion player and was able to play anything by ear. After Frank and Elsie were married they bought a big house in Scarborough but in 1935 moved back to York and opened a fish shop in the newly built Burnholme estate. Their two sons, Richard and Norman were born in York. Richard, the elder boy followed his father in the fish and chip business taking over the shop in Burnholme. The younger boy Norman, as well as having a musical career (stage name Steve Cassidy) became a teacher and eventually headmaster of St. George's School. The Lovely family ran the fish shop in the Groves until the 1940's when it was taken over by the Lawson family, relatives. The fish shop not only sold fish and chips to local residents but also supplied fish to hotels, restaurants and trains. During the war years the fish auctions were held at Beverley instead of Hull. There were often problems getting the fish in these years when petrol was scarce. They were only allocated a certain amount of fish. However the business survived during these years and thrived after the war. The shop only closed when the council made a compulsory purchase order on certain houses and shops in Penley's Grove street in the demolition of the 1960's. Only the breweries were allowed to keep their properties and even these were pulled down and rebuilt on the same site.

Mr Fowler remembered that some of the old houses in Jackson Street that were demolished in the 1960's were very small and there was only one WC and one tap for a certain number of houses. He remembered some of the characters that his parents talked about from their youth. One lady, they recalled was so annoyed by the noise made by late night revellers from the Reindeer pub that she once emptied the contents of her chamber pot on them. Sid Haw who owned a garage was bow-legged from riding motor bikes especially in the speedway races. One man who worked at Reynold's farm, at the corner of Lord Mayor's Walk and Gillygate, was a frequent visitor to the Unicorn public house. Rumour had it, that he was often the worse for drink but always arrived home safely, in his cart, as his horse knew its own way back to the farm.

Many immigrant families lived in Union Terrace in the early years of the 20th century, families like the Kaisers, Morris and Steigman. He remembered his aunt telling him that once, in the 1st World War, she had to pull Mrs Kaiser off the road and take her into her house to escape demonstrators against German families. He recalled that a Mr Tasker had been found dead in suspicious circumstances in a house in Providence Place. This house was well known as a gambling den and a lot of money changed hands here and it was often raided by the police.[3]

Mr Thompson's Memories
In the 1930's Mr Thompson lived with his mother and stepfather, John and Minnie Stubbs at the Dove Inn, Jackson Street. He was born in Walmgate were his father had a fruit shop. After his father died, when he was only young, his mother married again and they all went to live in the Groves. Mr Thompson remembered the games he played with his friends in the streets. Football was the most popular game, but marbles and a game with cigarette cards called "Knocky Down" were also played. He recalled some of the shopkeepers in the area. There was Dent's joiners, Mr Philip, hairdresser and Ossie Garrat who had a greengrocer's shop. Mr Marsden, Blackie, Spavin, Barker, Gunnell, Charlie Sunman, Pie Bean and Tom Harland were just some of his neighbours he remembered. The Rosser family were at the Bowling Green Inn before they moved to the Punch Bowl. Later Mr Thompson's family moved to the Bowling Green pub which was in Bowling Green Lane.[4]

Alderman Hutchinson's Memories
Mr C Hutchinson's grandfather, Charles Thorburn Hutchinson was Lord Mayor of York 1937/38. He lived at No. 12 Park Grove, was an active member of Groves Chapel and taught in the Sunday School there so he had a special interest in the Groves district. He also owned a grocery store and post office at the corner of St. Maurice's Road and Monkgate and one on Clarence Street. The one near Monk Bar was one of York's oldest post offices. When it opened it sold stamps bearing a picture of Queen Victoria. It closed in the 1960's and was scheduled for demolition under York's inner ring road scheme. When Alderman Hutchinson was elected in November 1937, one of his first duties was to help distribute food parcels to the unemployed. Four tons of tea, margarine, sugar

and liver were given out to unemployed people who had to queue in Exhibition Square. In December six hundred poor children were given a Xmas treat. They saw a western film, "Laramie" at the Grand cinema in Clarence Street and were given sweets and toys. Dolls and toys were distributed from the Lord Mayor's fund. A grocer's shop was reconstructed in a new street built in the Kirk Museum, called Hutchinson and Thompson. The sheriff of York that year was called Mr Thompson and was a grocer also. In January 1938 Alderman Hutchinson attended the pantomime organised by the Blue Coat School. Later that year he visited the Groves Methodist Chapel for their annual tea and social gatherings. He was also in attendance when the Rev. Cloudesley Shovel, a Methodist circuit Minister opened the Peckitt Street shelter for girls in need. Opening the new premises in Redeness Street for the York Boy's Club and attending the cup tie between York city and Huddersfield town were just some of his duties as Lord Mayor in 1938.[5]

St. Hilda's Home

The former Industrial School in Lowther Street became a local authority Home for children chargeable to the Public Assistance Committee in the early 1930's. Babies were sent to the Elms, Hull Road and older boys lived at another Home in Feversham Crescent.

The following are some abstracts from the Public Assistance Committee's minutes.

1936.

November.

Increase in small children at St. Hilda's. Twenty under seven. Children taken to Skipwith Common. Two boys opened St. Thomas's bazaar. Farm boy's Martimas Fair held at St. Hilda's. Children came from other areas.

1937.

June.

Holiday camp at Filey booked. Relay Wireless installed. One boy, D Crowther 13 years, helped to emigrate to Australia. Allowance for children boarded out, eight shillings plus extra for clothes. Two boys sent to Castle Howard farm school.

October.

Two boys placed at a farm at Skirpinbeck, Pocklington.

1939.

September.

Babies aged two to five years sent to a Home at Hovingham. Jean Byne boarded out. Many children incontinent, ruining mattresses and sheets.

Infants from St. Hilda's Home, 84 Lowther Street. Outing to Bridlington. c.1950.
(Courtesy of Mrs M Dyson)

1940.

February.

Youth bitten by a pig whilst in farm service to receive £5 compensation. County hospital fees paid out of this. Miss McGuire, Assistant Superintendent, Miss Clements, Foster Mother. Miss Dutton, seamstress.

July.

G Ellison entered Castle Howard farm. Arrangements made to evacuate children to Canada, America and New Zealand. Day's outing at Bishopthorpe Palace. Sixty children in the Home, eleven at Hovingham Lodge. Air raid shelters built in the garden at St. Hilda's.

1941

May. D Parker apprentice cook at Royal Station Hotel.

1942

May. Ivy Tattersfield started work at Betty's cafe. Fifteen shillings a week and meals. Dennis Barker lodging with his uncle in Leeman Road was bombed out, lost all his clothes.

1945

March.

Three costumes belonging to Miss Mcguire damaged by moths, reimbursed three guineas. One boy that had stolen a bicycle valued at six pounds sent to a Approved School.[6]

Wilfrid Cousin's Memories

Wilfrid Cousins grew up in St. Hilda's and the boy's Home in Feversham Crescent in the 1930's. He was told he had been left as a baby on the steps of The Elms, Hull Road wrapped in brown paper. He recalled his days in the Home when Miss Mcguire, later to become Mrs Milburn, was in charge. There were six boys in each dormitory and the older boys had to look after the younger ones. The boys always had to wash the dishes before they went out, Friday night was housework night and for this they wore hessian aprons. Mr Cousins remembered pushing a wheelbarrow to St. Hilda's to collect the groceries and then going to the workhouse for the bread that was baked there. It was always two enormous loaves. It was a very strict regime in the Home and the boys were punished for small misdemeanours. If you were very naughty you were sent to St. Hilda's for the cane. Bedwetting was punished by "having your nose rubbed in it". Sometimes the offenders were locked in the coal cellar for two to three hours Mr Cousins recalled. When the children from St. Hilda's were old enough to go to work the girls were mostly entered into domestic service and the boys into farm work. Mr Cousins went to a farm at Millington Heights, near Pocklington. He remembered that his days there were very hard and the farmer cruel. He along with other farm lads had to sleep in the stable and only went in the farmhouse for their Sunday dinners. He was glad when his time finished there and he could return to York. Later he was employed at Messrs Backhouse and sons in York and enjoyed his stay there much better.[7]

Margaret Dyson's Memories

Margaret Dyson entered St. Hilda's in the 1940's when she was only five years. She remembered being treated quite harshly when she was small. Each morning there was a punishment line and children were often caned for trivial offences. Those who had wet the bed were especially singled out and were humiliated in front of the other children. There was always lots of housework to be done such as floors to be washed and potatoes to be peeled. There was a rota for the washing up and two children had to wash the dishes for forty

Girls in garden of St. Hilda's Home. c.1950.
(Courtesy of Mrs M Dyson)

people. The girls slept in dormitories and the staff had a room at the end so they could keep an eye on their charges. One room had a little window to enable the staff to peer down at the girls. In spite of this they often had pillow fights and told each other ghost stories when lights were out Margaret recalled. This often resulted in a smack round the head or a wallop on the backside if caught. Sent to bed without tea or supper was another punishment for misbehaving.

Each Xmas there was a Xmas tree in the Common Room and Father Xmas visited the girls in their dormitories and each child received two presents. Margaret remembered that when she became a teenager it became embarrassing to have to sit up in bed with a large bow in her hair waiting to receive her presents from Father Xmas. In the summer months the children from St. Hilda's had two week's holiday at Primrose Valley. They lived in tents and had a little more freedom than when they were in the Home. Each child had a set of holiday clothes, shorts, tea-shirts and sandals. After the holiday these clothes were put away for the next year. When the clothes became too small they were passed down to another child. The usual clothes for every day wear in the Home was a flannel vest, liberty bodice and open drawers The girl's hair was always cut in same style. When Miss McGuire became the Matron things began to improve Margaret recalled. The school was very involved with St. Thomas's Church in Lowther Street and Sundays were mostly spent at Sunday School and at the church services there. When Margaret was older she joined the Girl's Friendly Society belonging to the church. Once she remembered one girl from the Home putting 3d in the collection and taking out 2d for change.

Margaret remembered the houses and shops that were in the Groves area when she was young. Pocket money was spent at Mrs Paige's shop in Lowther Street. She recalled the small houses in Jackson Street and the blacksmith's shop, Pulleyn at the end of Garden Street. There were big gates leading into St. Hilda's and a large garden at the back. However the children were only allowed in this on special occasions. When Margaret became a teenager she was fostered out to Mr and Mrs Tom Mooring who lived in Lockwood Street and spent many a happy weekend with them and their daughter. Mrs Mooring is now a widow and well in her eighties but Margaret still visits her regularly.[8]

Nellie Mooring's Memories

Mrs Mooring, née Atkin, lived in Lockwood Street in the 1930's and 1940's. Her husband, Tom Mooring had lived in Garden Street when he was young. He started at St. Thomas's School when he was four. When the boys were eight they had to go to the Manor School and there were only girls after that age at St. Thomas's. Mrs Mooring remembered the families that lived near her when she was first married. In Garden Street there was the Holt, Potter, Hughes, Dawes, ledger, Balderson and Gilligan families. She remembered that Mr Holt worked at the Co-op in March Street and Mrs Curtis had a cat called "Get". She also

Garden Street, George V. Silver Jubilee 1935. *(Courtesy of Mrs N Morring)*

recalled a family that lived nearby, the father had died of pneumonia because it was rumoured his wife refused to wash and dry his clothes properly.

Before Mrs Mooring was married she had worked at the County Hospital in Monkgate. She had started work as a scullery maid in the kitchens with a starting wage of £1.7s.5d. Eventually she became the assistant cook. The head cook was called Miss Lees. It was very hard work in the kitchens then. The pans were iron and very heavy she recalled. The kitchens were all underground and all the stone floors and corridors had to be scrubbed every day. She remembered a woman employed just to scrub the floors. The Matron would come down to the kitchens to discuss the menus every day with the cook. Most of the food was steamed and she particularly remembered cabbage was always on the menu. Everybody had to have porridge in a morning, there wasn't much choice then. Sunday morning there was always fried polony from Wright's butchers. The private patients had a more varied and different menu. The Matron would always carve the chicken for the private patients Mrs Mooring recalled. The nurses did some of the cooking for patients on special diets there wasn't any dieticians then. She remembered diabetic patients having to have just tripe, no potatoes. Next to the kitchens was the storeroom where ice, which was used to stop bleeding, was stored, which was wrapped in blankets for use during the night. Blocks of ice were purchased from the fishmongers. Farmers would bring in eggs and vegetables, which were stored until needed in this storeroom. The X-ray room was along the corridor from the kitchens. The patients were brought down to this room which was always kept dark. The morgue was in this area also and bodies were brought down in the lift near the kitchens. They were laid out on trestle tables and just covered with a sheet, she recalled.

Mrs Nellie Mooring, née Atkin and Miss Lees, Cook at County Hospital. c.1930. *(Courtesy of Mrs N Mooring)*

The gates of the hospital were closed and locked at night and if the nurses and kitchen staff were not back by a certain time, they were locked out. Once when Mrs Mooring was young she was late back from a party and could not get back into her room in the hospital. She stopped the night with some friends in a cottage in St. Maurice's Road but had to sneak in the milk gate before six. She remembered some of the staff who worked with her in these days. The Matron was a Miss Steele and always had a maid to help her dress. Mrs Horsman and a Mrs Tamms were in charge over the laundry, Alfie Rush was the gardener and Harold Binns and Bill Hudson were just two of the many porters employed at the hospital then. Although the work was very hard and the regime strict Mrs Mooring enjoyed her time there and missed the laughter and banter among the kitchen staff when she left.[9]

Brian Sargent's Memories

Mr Brian Sargent remembered some of the shopkeepers in the Groves area when he was a lad living in Vyner Street. He particularly recalled visiting Charlie Nicholson who had his hairdresser's shop in Lowther Street. He was a veteran of the trenches in World War One. The appalling conditions in France had left him with chronically ulcerated feet and ankles, which had to be always bandaged and forced him to wear carpet slippers. He was always in pain but bore it all without hardly any complaint. As he was unable to hold down a conventional job he had opened a modest hairdressing salon in his front parlour of his house. He had a chair that swivelled round so he could cut his customer's hair without rising up too much, all the while keeping up a cheerful chatter. Mr Sargent and his father were full of admiration for him.

Another shop that Mr Sargent enjoyed visiting in his youth was Mr Fred Fenton's cycle shop, at 81 to 83 Clarence Street. Altogether his family had bought six bicycles from Mr Fenton, and to a young boy this shop was a fascinating place to visit. In addition to the cycles and components on display and characteristic oily smell, there were storage benches lined with closed packed rows of wireless accumulators, gently fizzing and bubbling, left by local people for recharging at a few coppers a time. Much more exciting though were the times when Mr Sargent called to take possession of a brand new machine. Fred would disappear down a long dark corridor and reappear a few moments later wheeling a new bicycle, his face wreathed in smiles, glowing with pride at his workmanship.

The sweet shop at the corner of Monkgate and Penley Grove Street was another magnet to Mr Sargent as young boy. Once he had sixpence to spend and set off from chapel for this shop, full of anticipation of the lovely things he could buy with this money. However as he approached the shop he saw a man sitting on the kerbside begging for money for food. He reached the open doorway of the shop and then had a fit of conscience, ran back and dropped the precious sixpence into the man's receptive cap. Afterwards, instead of feeling happy about his good deed he sloughed home, despising himself for being a fool.[10]

Groves Working Men's Club

Groves Working Men's Club started its days officially in the 1900's in premises in Abbott Street in the "Tin Tabernacle" but then known as Haxby Road Working

Men's Club. Older members believe that the very first premises used were in White Cross Road a few years earlier but no records exist of this. Some of the first members were J Fowler, Tom Mooring, Tom Scott and J Tuthill.

In 1919, the club moved to Settrington House, in Penley's Grove Street. This was a spacious house with a long lawn and an imposing drive up to the front door. These assets attracted a lot of visitors for there was ample parking space for charabancs calling in from the coast. Parties of rugby supporters made the Groves Club their rendezvous also when their team was visiting York at Clarence Street.

Clarence Street

In these early days, T Ashwell, T Burke, G Halliday, Ernie Harton, Bill Jennings, G Petch, Charle Rich and Tom Stonehouse were just some of the men who helped to make this club a success. Family ties were strong and the Bucknell, Howes, Mooring and Robson families were well represented. In 1930, alterations were made at the club house. The ground floor was converted into one large room with seating accommodation and three billiard tables. Billiards was a pastime this club excelled in.

At the end of World War Two, annual walking matches were started. These were a great social occasion with a band playing to members and their families on the lawn. A popular sport in the club was angling and Walter Pink was the secretary in the forties and early fifties. Other committee members at this time were, A Darnborough, F Hudson, B Lynch, T Mooring, P Scrimshire, C Tolson and C Woodley. Tom Brown was the secretary and Eric Bradley the steward.[11]

Clarence Working Men's Club

This club was founded in 1898 in a room over a hair dressing salon at 95 Clarence Street. It was the second club in York to be affiliated to the national Club and Institute Union, (Leeman Road Working Men's Club was the first). Another room in the same building was acquired for use as a billiards room and the club stayed in these premises until after the 1st World War when the property next door was taken over.

In 1927, the present building in Clarence Street was opened for which members raised a record £3,500. The club has always been known for its great sporting achievements. 1928 was an especially good year when the Clarence Street bowlers won many competitions. Clarence Gardens, opened in June 1909 and the new bowling greens were ready for use later that year. Fishing was another popular pastime, Taff limbert was responsible for organising and playing in the fishing matches for many years. Bill Noakes, Tom King and S. Burdett were important members of the fishing section in these early days.

Trip from Groves Club. c.1950. (*Courtesy of Mr Myers*)

The old Groves United team, an outstanding amateur rugby team had its headquarters at this club in the early years but suffered from the loss of many players in the 1st World War and was later disbanded. In the forties and fifties, Clarence had two rugby teams. It was a fruitful nursery for senior clubs especially York City. York trainer, Billy Mills, was a former Clarence player and the pre-war team once went through five seasons unbeaten. S. Bardy, "Shacker" Batterby, Eric Bradley, W. Hodgson, "Moggy" Jackson, Norman Watling and "Tich" Wheatley were all players or members involved with the rugby at this club just after the war.

Although sport played a large part in this club, it was also involved with other activities. Social and educational outings, debates, quiz contests and concerts. 'Sick Clubs', benefits for pensioners and support for several convalescent homes around the country.

'Ike' Ankers, E. Gilligan, Tom Howden, F. Kirby, Ted Rhodes, Walt Smith and Sam Wilcock were just some of the men that helped to run this club in the early 1950's. The club is still flourishing today.[12]

Clarence Street Working Men's Club. First premises 94 Clarence Street, over the barber's shop. *(Courtesy of Y.E.P.)*

Chapter VI. Notes and References.
1. Memories of Mrs R Webster, 176. Askam Lane.
2. Information supplied by Mrs Morton, Heworth and Mrs Audrey Ewing.
3. Information supplied by Mr R Fowler, Heworth Green.
4. Memories of Mr Thompson, Muncaster.
5. Information supplied by Mr Hutchinson, Forest Way.
6. Y.C.A. Public Assistance Committee Reports (1935-45).
7. Information supplied by York Oral History Group.
8. Memories of Mrs Margaret Dyson, Wetherby.
9. Information supplied by Mrs N. Mooring, nËe, Atkin, Ashley Park.
10. Memories of Mr B. Sargent, Norwich.
11. Y.E.P. 1952.
12. Ibid. 1952.

Trip from the Reindeer Pub. c.1930. *(Courtesy of D. Poole)*

CHAPTER VII
WAR YEARS

Preparing For War

Although York was not bombed as much as neighbouring cities like Hull, Newcastle and Manchester it still experienced some air raids in the Second World War. There were eleven air strikes in which high explosives and incendiary bombs were dropped. The Groves area, just like the other areas in York had to prepare itself for air raids. There were numerous air raid shelters erected and a warden's post in Amber Street and one at the Grey Coat school in Monkgate.[1] The Air Raids Precaution Department visited Park Grove School in May of 1939 to decide what precautions would have to be taken in the event of war. The ceilings of certain rooms would have to be strengthened and these classrooms sand bagged. It was decided that all children above the age of seven on the premises during an air raid would be taken by the teachers to these rooms. Children below the age of seven to be sent home (hopefully before any bombing started!). Later in the year the number of air raid shelters were increased from two to six. On September the 1st(just two days before war was officially declared) the school was closed "on account of the impending emergency" On October 9th notices were sent out informing the children that they should commence half-time school. Later third year pupils to attend full time, 2nd years, afternoon's only and 1st years mornings only[2]

Rationing and Ration Books

Petrol rationing was introduced in 1939, food rationing began in January 1940 and clothes in 1941. Everyone was issued with a ration book and had to register at a provision's shop. The main food office, where ration books were obtained, was in Blake street, at the Assembly Rooms. Mr Elsegood remembered having to go there every week to collect two tins of National Dried Milk and a bottle of concentrated orange juice, for his mother. In 1940 at Park Grove School the Domestic centre was inspected to see if it could be used for community feeding if the district became homeless through air raids. In December of that year 5700 ration cards were filled in by one hundred of Park Groves best scholars. They were checked by the teachers and collected by the postman. A teacher took another 4000 filled up cards and unused ration books to the Food Office. These having been arranged in alphabetical order of the third letter of the surname.

Meat was particularly scarce during the war years. Mr Elsegood recalled that some butchers in the Groves area would write the name of the meat available that day on the shop's mirror. Everyone had to wait to be served in turn, alphabetically according to their surnames. His family were lucky as Elsegood was near the beginning of the alphabet, but those whose surnames were further down the alphabet had a long wait.[3]

End of Cole Street near Brook Street School. The spire of St. Thomas's Church can be seen in the distance. *(Courtesy of Mr R lake)*

Air Raids

On the 16th of January 1941, an air raid on York affected the Groves area. A newspaper article described it as a two hour raid on a north east town. Though about one hundred incendiary bombs and a number of high explosives were dropped in the course of a few hours, only three people were taken to hospital. They lived in a house with a shop attached and their premises received a direct hit.[4] This was the house and grocer's shop belonging to Mr Harold Bond at the end of Brownlow Street. Mr Bond had just come downstairs to investigate a little noise when suddenly a mighty explosion occurred. He had almost reached the bottom of the stairs when the front door was blown in on him. and he received serious stomach wounds. His eight year old daughter, who had followed him down, dived quickly under the table and escaped injury. Two other daughters, Clara and Audrey were later treated at the hospital for superficial wounds and shock. Unfortunately their father died two days later in hospital from his injuries. During this raid other minor casualties were dealt with at first aid posts.[5]

Damage

Three churches in this area, a public house, a children's Home and several private houses were also damaged. Park Grove School had several windows broken in the blast that came from the bomb dropped in Dudley Street. Thanks to the efficiency of the fire fighting arrangements the incendiary bombs were dealt with quickly and no serious outbreaks of fire occurred. Another bomb had fallen on a hut in the Groves area containing valuable wireless apparatus belonging to a wireless enthusiast serving with the Royal Navy. His loss was estimated at £200. Another serious financial loss was felt by a pig breeder in the area. Blast and flying bricks wrecked his sties, killing seven of his stock valued at £50.

One of the luckiest people in this district was Mrs Wales, aged ninety, who was asleep when a bomb fell in her kitchen. Children in the area seemed to have been unperturbed by the loud explosions and many slept through them. Eight year old Doreen Flanagan's main concern was for the safety of her beloved doll and another nine year old was frightened in case his canary in the sitting room had been killed in the blast. One woman whose house, with its shattered window panes and curtains left blowing in the breeze, was typical of scores of others. She said the first she knew of the bombing was a flash like lightning near the window. She attributed the noise to the neighbours next door but was quickly disillusioned by her husband. "Never mind, our thumbs are up and we are still alive", she said with a smile.[6]

In another raid on York on 17th December 1942 there was damage to Park Grove School and the Gas Works. In the school log books of that time it was reported that several rooms were burnt out. The workshop and the other rooms were saved by the quick attention to fire bombs by the firewatchers. Thirty nine incendiary bombs fell in the yards in addition to those on the roofs. The school was flooded with water and the pupils were sent home until January 4th. The rest of December was used to clear up and salvage what could be saved. Three girl's classes were removed to Shipton Street. The school reopened on the 4th of January 1943 with no light and little heat. The five damaged rooms had no roof and snow and rain poured through these rooms and those below rendering them useless. Later temporary corrugated iron roofs were put over rooms seven to ten but for some unknown reason not over room six.[7]

Memories of Air Raids

Mrs Ros remembered that there was no school the next day when Park Grove School was bombed. Her family had gone into the nearest shelter, but had had to wait until it was unlocked by the night watchman. This poor man suffered from "Trench feet" which was the result of his time in the trenches in the First World War and he could only shuffle along very slowly. Mrs Ros thought they might all have been killed before they could get into the shelter if a bomb had dropped near them.[8] Mr Woodcock remembered going to Park Grove School the morning after this raid. Windows had all been blown out and the school was full of water he recalled. Next day when he went to school he was told to throw all the wet books out of the windows.[9] Mr Sargent remembered that a member of Monkgate Choir, Mr Amos Watson was returning from choir practice with his wife on the evening of this raid when the siren began to sound. They hurried along to their house at 75 Monkgate, which they had almost reached when they heard the drone of bomber's engines. They had just opened the front door when Amos was flung forward by the violence of the blast from the gas work's bomb. When he picked himself up, mercifully unharmed, he could not find the hat he had been wearing. It had just vanished and no amount of searching could reveal it. It was not until Spring cleaning time the following year that it was discovered neatly perched out of sight on top of the grandfather clock in the hall where the blast had carried it.[10]

Mr Elsegood recalled that the Blue Coat School on Peasholme Green was damaged that night by incendiary bombs. The stables were set alight and all the boys had to stand in the gardens and form a chain to pass fire buckets.[11] Mrs Bamford remembered seeing the sky all lit up when the station was bombed in the Baedeker raid in April 1942. Her family who lived in Penley's Grove Street had a Morrison shelter erected in the front room. Sometimes the neighbors would share this shelter with them. One neighbour, Mrs Bamford recalled, was rather large and took up all the room in the shelter, often there was no room for the rest of them.[12] Mr Elsegood recalled that during the war years he delivered newspapers from Dunwell's shop on Clarence Street, to the Clifton area. He remembered that on the day after the York Blitz he had to return most of them because the houses had gone, bombed, in the previous night's raid.

Holidays At Home

As people were unable to go away on holiday during the War years the government organised schemes for "Holidays at Home". Some of the schools remained open during the summer holidays and the teachers worked on a rota basis.

Mrs Fairclough remembered that Park Grove School opened in the School holidays for any child that wished to attend. There were woodwork, metalwork, singing and country dancing classes. Out door activities included swimming, long walks and cycle rides. Milk and school dinners were also provided. Mrs Fairclough also recalled picking rose hips, for Rose Hip Syrup and collecting jam jars, for the National Jam Making effort.[13]

During the war years when most of the able bodied men were away fighting extra help was always needed on the farms. The October holiday was always known as potato picking week and most children over 12 years went potato picking if they could, to earn some pocket money. Outside the Groves chapel was the place most people remembered. as where they had to stand to be picked up to be taken to the farms near York. The author remembered going with her friend who lived in the Groves to pick potatoes at a farm near Pocklington. The weather in October always seemed to be very cold and frosty in a morning but later becoming warmer, typical Autumn weather. The children were placed in gangs and had to walk behind the tractor and spinner and pick up the exposed potatoes and place into buckets. These were loaded into carts pulled by horses. The work was hard and very back breaking especially for "towny" children and the dinner of bread and cheese and mugs of tea to wash it down, brought by the farmer's wife, was always very welcome. The author, determined not to be labelled as a "towny" and also to impress the local farm lads, jumped on the back of a farm horse for a bet. The horse immediately galloped off over the rough fields, with the author hanging on for grim death, (never been on a horse before) much to the amusement of the farm lads. However her prowess (or not) on a horse must have impressed as the next morning one of these farm lads appeared on a tractor at her home in York, to ask for a date, which was of course promptly refused.[14] Mr Elsegood also remembered going pea pulling and carrot weeding in the summer holidays at farms around Full Sutton, as well as potato picking in October.[15] The log books of Park Grove School reported that in 1943, certain boys were to have an extra fortnight off school for potato picking owing to the bad weather in the October half term.

V.E. Celebrations

Victory in Europe was announced on the 7th May 1945. There were great celebrations all over the country. Every area in every town organised its own street party. Even though food was still rationed, everyone made a special effort and contributed something, especially home-made sandwiches and cakes. There was jelly, ice-cream and "pop" for the children, and large quantities of tea, made in large urns. Flags and bunting decorated the houses and streets. Chairs were taken outside and long tables set-up. Fortunately it was a fine day.

There were many street parties in the Monkgate and Groves area. Mrs Cole remembered the one held in Townend Street. There were fancy dress competitions and games and races for all age groups. She recalled that her mother, Mrs Wheatley, fell in a race and received a black eye.[16] One lady remembered the combined party of Eldon Street, and Eldon Terrace, when all the children received a mug inscribed with "V.E. 1945". Public houses ran out of beer as singing and dancing continued long into the night. Celebrations were held on V.J. night, three months later, but not on such a grand scale.

Ladies from Townend Street. *(Courtesy of Mrs M Cole)*

Chapter VII. Notes and References.
1. Y.R.L. Yorkshire County Council *2nd World War document pack.*
2. Y.C.A. Park Grove *Log Books*
3. Information supplied by Mr B Elsegood, Moatfield York.
4. Y.E.P. 1941.
5. Information supplied by Mrs G Hall, Hempland Avenue.
6. Y.E.P. 1941
7. Park Grove *Log books.* 1939-1945.
8. Memories of Mrs Ros, Huntington.
9. Information supplied by Mr D Woodcock, Moatfield.
10. Information supplied by Mr B. Sargent, Norwich.
11. Memories of Mr B Elsegood, Moatfield, Osbaldwick.
12. Information supplied by Mrs Bamford, Penley's Grove Street.
13. Memories of Mrs C Fairclough, Whitby Drive.
14. Memories of Author, Mrs A Appleton née Reeder.
15. Information supplied by Mr B Elsegood, Moatfield, Osbaldwick.
16. Memories of Mrs M Cole. Townend Street.

V.E. Party Mansfield Place.

V.E. Party Park Grove School.

V.E. Party Townend Street.

CHAPTER VIII
MEMORIES OF THE 1940s & 1950s

Mr Lake's Memories

Mr Robin Lake was born in 1935 in Garden Street. This house had a special toilet at the bottom of the yard. The adult toilet was enclosed with panelled wood with a small one next to it for a child, perhaps it had once been an old privy. Next to his house was a yard, King's rag yard. He remembered the night watch man who once fell asleep with his feet on an old pot bellied stove and burnt them very badly. There was also pig sties in this yard. He remembered quite a few people that kept pigs in the Groves, Jack Merrick had sties and there were more pig sties opposite Rhode's were the animals were slaughtered. Mr Lake started work in Ridsdale's butcher's shop in the 1940's and he remembered

Geoff Lake and his father, with a hand-operated crane. c.1940.
(Courtesy of lake Family)

some of the people who lived in the Groves then. He recalled that Jim Pulleyn had a blacksmith's shop at the end of March Street where he kept shire horses and cattle were often slaughtered at the back of the butcher's shops. He recalled Atkinson's pot shop, Lea's bakery, old man Slater, Richardson's sweet shop and Questa's ice-cream shop. When he was a lad he would love to go into the latter shop just to hear the owners ask him in their Italian accent if he wanted a "Furry penny or sixxy penny" ice. When he was in charge of the butcher's shop in Penley's Grove Street he recalled a lady who came in the shop to buy meat for her neighbours. She was very efficient and wrote the price of everything down in a book with a pencil with a silver top. This pencil was one she had used with a dance card when she was young, she told Mr Lake. Her father had insisted that she did not dance too much with one person and would inspect this book. However she admitted she had often altered it.

People would generally use the shops in the area were they lived and didn't go further a field. Inhabitants were also wary of been seen using shops in another area. Lads from Union Terrace, which was just off Clarence Street, would not venture through the Groves to go for cinders from the Gas Works, if they could help it, for fear of being attacked by Groves lads. Mr Lake remembered some of the public houses in the area. There was the Magpie, once called Magpie and Stump in Penley's Grove Street, Cross Keys, just past March Street the Reindeer, just past the end of Abbott Street, and the Castle Howard Ox, at the end of Townend Street. Another small pub called The Trumpet once stood in Townend Street opposite the Church, but was closed in 1908. There was also the Punch Bowl, at the end of Lowther Street, the Dove, in Jackson Street and the Bowling Green Inn at the end of Bowling Green Lane. He recalled that when he was young, women were not allowed in the bars of public houses. He remembered seeing old Mrs Theaker with her cronies sitting in the kitchen of the Magpie public house, singing away. Their husbands would be in the bar, possibly playing dominoes, occasionally checking that their wives had their bottles of Guinness or milk stout.[1]

Mrs Ros's Memories

Mrs Denise Ros, née Simpson, lived in St. John's Street when she was a girl. Her mother had been married three times but then was left on her own to bring up seven children, so they were very poor. She recalled they often had to put coats on the bed to keep warm in the winter. Her mother cleaned at the College for Girls on a Thursday night but only received a small wage and had to pay 6d for a bucket of hot water from a nearby shop. Mrs Ros remembered some of the shopkeepers in the Groves area in the 1940's. She loved Richardson's sweetshop with its arrowroot and liquorice sticks, and Dowling's bread shop, with its fresh bread cakes and thinly cut ham. She also recalled, Skinner's hairdresser's, Flatley's off licence and a Mrs Fourbert, who had a shop in Groves Lane.

Magpie Public House. c.1950. Demolished 1960, rebuilt on same site.
(Courtesy of Y.C.A)

Mrs Ros attended Park Grove School in the 1940's and recalled some of the teachers. There was a Miss Shillitoe, Miss Tate and Miss Watson. One teacher was keen on making her pupils march and giving them lots of compositions to write. Once she gave them five to do all at once. Mrs Ros's mother was often given second hand clothes for her children to wear. Her daughter thought she was the only child in the school that wore Queen Ann uniform and was often singled out for wearing pink knickers for P. T. when the regulation colour was navy blue. Mrs Ros believed that in those days poor children were often shown up by the teachers. She recalled how one boy who was often late, because he had to help his father before school, was caned, on his hands, even though they were frozen. One lad was regularly told to "pull up his socks" but when he did this, there were no feet in them. Mrs Ros remembered some of her school friends. There was Colin Smithson, who she recalled as, "a bit of a rogue" and Alan Jarvis who was always fighting. She remembered Charline Phillips, who lived in Brownlow Street and the Winteringham family, who had a clothes shop along Clarence Street. There was also a boy called Wrigglesworth, who had ginger hair, his parents had a grocer's shop at the corner of Waverley Street. Rita and Andy Brody, Eileen Beavis who lived in Bearpark Square and Jean Nugent, her parents were once the landlords of the Bowling Green pub, were just some of the school friends she remembered.

Mrs Ros also recalled some of her neighbours. There was Mr Farmery who lived opposite the Magpie pub, who made pictures out of small pieces of glass and a Mr Henry Major, who always wore leggings. Mr Elliott was a night watch man. His father had been in the navy and his mother could not cope with all her children, so he was brought up in the Blue Coat charity school. She remembered the pre-fabs that were situated near were the D.H.S. building is now and St. Maurice 's Church before it was demolished in the 1960's.[2]

Mr Myers with Park Grove Club Committee members. c.1950. *(Courtesy of Mr Myers)*

Mr Myers's Memories

Mr Frank Myers took over the grocer's shop at the corner of Park Crescent and Bowling Green Lane in 1946. The previous owners were the Jackson family. In those days there were lots of houses nearby and there was a good trade even though there were many other shops in the area. There were sixty four houses in nearby Jackson Street. Dent's joinery works, at the end of Park Crescent, employed forty men, who often came into the shop for sweets and cigarettes. Children would call in the shop on their way to Park Grove or St. Wilfrid's School. The shop opened 8am-6pm weekdays and 10-12am on Sunday mornings. At other times people would often knock on the door or window if they had run out of essentials. Most people shopped locally then and would call in the shop three or four times a day instead of getting a big order weekly. Some people would purchase goods on "tick" but always paid up at the end of the week. Mr Myers believed that people were more honest in those days and he never had any trouble with petty pilfering or the shop broken into. During the war years, the shop was rationed with Crow's wholesalers for groceries and Clark's for cigarettes. Mr Myers sold Players, Woodbines and Robin cigarettes, 2d for five and 4d for twenty. Everything was weighed out then and Mr Myers boned his own bacon and rolled joints of ham. Most men worked at the Railway or Rowntree's factory. There were plenty of jobs to be had in the 1950's, Mr Myers recalled. Before the demolition of many of the houses, the Groves was one of the busiest areas of York. Mr Myers remembered some of his neighbours. There was big Jim Benson he had the cycle shop in Lowther Street, Mr Nicholson, hairdresser, Arthur Fowler he was a chimney sweep and Charlie Dixon who was the landlord of the Bowling Green Inn. Edward Goldsborough had the off-licence nearby and Charlie Rich delivered newspapers. He also recalled a lady called Evelyne, who sold fruit and vegetables from her front room of her house in Park Crescent. In the summer she would display her goods outside her front door. He remembered Jack Curry who drove a delivery lorry and a man called Albert. His wife was very keen on backing horses he recalled. Mr Myers did not remember any serious fights or trouble in the area when the police had to be called out. He said that there was often a few fights between men when they had had too much to drink but all was forgotten when they had sobered up next morning.

Shepherd's Shop, corner of Mansfield Place and Townend Street. c. 1950
(Courtesy of Y.C.A.)

Mr Myers was involved with Groves Working Men's Club for over fifty years serving as President, social secretary and steward. At one time he thought that this club was the best in York. Good acts were acquired for Saturday and Sunday nights, some of the people have become famous TV stars. Jim Davidson was a regular, as was Stan Richards who now plays Seth Armstrong in the TV soap, "Emmerdale". These stars would only cost £5 or £10 in those days. There was also good prices for the Bingo or "Housey Housey" as it was originally known. The Club also organised Xmas parties and trips to the seaside for member's children. Although the Club has been renovated in the last few years, Mr Myers thought that attendances had fallen away. This was partly due to the fact that many people were moved away when some of the old houses were demolished and young people preferred to patronise the town pubs.[3]

Mr and Mrs Marshall's Memories

Mr Noel Marshall was brought up in the Groves in the 1940's and 1950's. He lived with his grandparents for many years whilst his parents went to work in London. His grandmother, Mrs Shepherd had a second hand shop in Mansfield Place. She liked to call it an antique shop but she bought and sold anything and everything. If you took in two comics you could only get one different comic back. She was thought to be Jewish, by her neighbours, as she was well known to drive a hard bargain. Mr Marshall remembered some of the characters that lived in the area in his youth. There was Charlie Thornton who delivered papers, Mr Nicholson and Mr Rutherford, barbers, and Mr Kidd who mended shoes. There was also a Mr Ash who had a bookie's shop in Silver Street. His mother lived next door and always had a canary in the window. Slater's chemist made up their own yellow mixture. Mr Marshall recalled that his mother always gave him a teaspoonful of some black liquorice mixture, on a Friday night, which she said, was a treat, but he realised now, was Syrup of Figs. In the summer months he would play football in the square with his friends, but if the ball hit Mr Richardson's window, he would come out of his house in a fine rage and chase them all away. His mother peeled potatoes for Syke's fishshop on a Friday, so on that day, they would have free fish and chips.

Mrs Pat Marshall, née Robinson, was born at 35 Lowther Street, which was opposite the entrance to Bedford Street. She was the youngest of the family of five girls and one boy. Her house was only a "two up and two down" with a scullery and a backyard. Her parents slept in one bedroom and the girls in another, her brother slept on a camp bed in the front room. In the girl's bedroom there was a double and a single bed. The eldest girl had the single bed until she left home and then the next one in line moved into it. Because Mrs Marshall was the youngest she had the bedroom all to herself, for a little while, before she was married. Her father, Frank Robinson, was a local boxer in the 1930's. He fought at the Empire and the Rialto. His entrance was always accompanied by the tune "Old Soldiers Never Die".

Mrs Marshall remembered some of her neighbours when she was growing up in the Groves. There was Mrs McCloud from Bedford Street, she was always up early delivering milk on a bicycle with a basket on the front, Mr Nicholson, hairdresser, who carried on his business from his front room. She remembered once being dragged by her mother to his shop to have her long plaits cut off. There were often disputes between neighbours over the positioning of dustbins Mrs Marshall recalled. Some neighbours were very inquisitive and spent a lot of time peeping out from behind lace curtains, watching people's comings and goings. Anybody who acquired a reputation for "entertaining gentlemen friends" was the object of much observation and speculation and supplied fuel for the gossips who often collected at street corners. There was no TV or "Coronation Street" to watch, in those days, it was all happening in the streets. On a Sunday morning the Salvation Army would play at each corner of the area, and the children would sing and march to the music. Rag and bone men, who gave goldfish in a jam jar for a few old clothes, the knife grinder and the tingalary man with his organ and monkey were frequent visitors.

In the summer months, Mrs Marshall would play in the streets with the other children. Games, such as skipping and hopscotch were very popular. A long washing line was extended across the streets and every one could join in. In the winter months, she remembered going to the gas works with an old pram or box on wheels to collect cinders, which would last longer than coal, on the fires. In November, all the children from each street would join together to collect refuse for a big bonfire. However, in the winter months when it had been snowing, there was friendly rivalry among the children from Lowther street and Jackson Street. A big barricade of snow was built at each end of the street which was used to hide behind or as a barricade to fire snowballs at rival gangs. She did not remember any serious fights taking place in the Groves when she was young. Most children were frightened of policemen and the wrath of their parents to misbehave. She was threatened with being sent to "the Marmalade Home" which was what the Industrial School in Lowther Street was called, if she was very naughty[4]

Mr Martindale's Memories

Mr Alan Martindale was born at 59 Brownlow Street in 1935. His mother died when he was only eleven and his aunts, who lived in Diamond Street, kept a motherly eye on him whilst he was growing up. His father eventually re-married and he acquired two stepbrothers and later his father and stepmother had twin boys. Mr Martindale remembered playing football and cricket in the back lane between Brownlow Street and Eldon Street. He also remembered some of the shopkeepers nearby. There was Bond's grocer's shop at the corner of Dudley Street, Mr Precious who had a shop in Neville Terrace, Swan's the milk people and Mr Barber the barber. He also remembered the Halliwell family, they had

Robinson family. 35 Lowther Street. *(Courtesy of Mrs P Marshall)*

built a wooden extension at the back of their house to keep pigeons. His parents were friendly with Mr and Mrs Garrett who had a greengrocer's shop in Lowther Street. "Ossie" Garrett, as he was known, was in the Observer Corps during the 2nd world War, based at Heslington Hall, and Mr Martindale recalled that "Ossie" was always drumming messages in Morse code on the table. Whilst his father was away during the war he and his mother would often share the Morrison shelter erected in the Garrat's house and he recalled that once "Ossie" had carried him home on his shoulders after an air raid. Mr Martindale recalled the bad flooding that occurred in York in 1947. The water from the River Foss "came right across" Huntington Road and the Army had to ferry people in flat bottom boats across the road from the end of Lowther Street to Monkgate. When Mr Martindale became a teenager he joined Centenary Methodist youth club.[5]

Mr Elsegood's Memories

Mr Brian Elsegood lived at 78 Penley's Grove Street in the 1930's and 40's. His first school was St. Thomas's School, in Lowther Street. He remembered that once he had climbed up on the roof of the school when playing Hide and Seek with his friends and hit his head on the school bell. In 1941, because his father was at war and his mother was working at the laundry in Peaseholme Green, he and his brother were placed in the Blue Coat School. He hated his days there.

He recalled that the regime in the School was very strict and you were caned for the smallest misdemeanour. He particularly remembered the bullying that went on and how the older boys, especially the prefects, tormented the smaller ones. Because Mr Elsegood was only eight years old when he was entered into the school, he was often at the receiving end of all this, but was threatened that worse would befall him if he told. He recalled that many boys attempted to run away but were always brought back by the police and punished, by the teachers.

One highlight of Mr Elsegood's time at the School was when all the boys were invited to the Mansion House for tea, (23rd June 1943) when William Thompson was Lord Mayor. Mr Thompson had been at the Blue Coat School also.

Another momentous occasion Mr Elsegood remembered, was when the Mount School girls played host to the boys and organised games and a wonderful tea. Normally the meals in the Blue Coat School were very sparse and the lads often had to eat stale crusts.

In 1944, Mr Elsegood's father came home on leave and took him and his brother out of the School. To a small boy, who up to the time he entered that School, had only known a normal home environment, it had been a very traumatic experience. He felt very sorry for all the lads he left behind.

Mr Elsegood remembered most of the small shops that were near his house in Penley's Grove Street. He recalled when young he spent a lot of time looking for cigarettes for his father, who was a heavy smoker. After the war cigarettes were still in short supply and he and his brother would have to find out which shop

Atkinson's Hardware Store and yard, Penley's Grove Street. c.1950. *(Courtesy of Y.C.A.)*

had some in stock. He also had to collect his father's Sunday paper from Mr Millard's shop in Garden Street. On Saturdays, he would tie sticks in bundles for Mr Atkinson and received 6d for this. He also had to collect cinders from the Gas Works, being stopped on one occasion, by an old lady who persuaded him to sell his cinders to her, because she had a sick husband. When Mr Elsegood returned to the Gas Works for his load, he found he was too late and it was closed. His father did not believe his tale and broke his cart. However the old lady turned out to be his mother's friend, so all ended well.

Mr Elsegood also recalled that Bill Fairless, who was the publican of the Castle Howard Ox in the 1930's, was a huge man. He weighed at least twenty-three or twenty-four stone and always kept so many pint glasses in his waistcoat pocket. He sat at a special table with a piece carved out of it to accommodate his large bulk. Mr Farmery, who had a shop in Penley Grove Street had a dreadful impediment Mr Elsegood recalled. He also remembered Mr Paylor who was deaf and dumb, Billy Bearpark who was blind, Kitty Hicks, who always visited the Magpie pub with a jug and the Theakstone, Bevan, Gainley, Vasher and Paxton families. Mr Elsegood belonged to the Boy's Brigade when he was young and learned to signal with flags. They would practice at the back of the Groves Chapel he recalled.

Mr Elsegood's house in Penley's Grove Street was rented from the Lane family who had a shop and coal business next door. Once, it was decided by Mr Lane, that the Elsegood's front room should be used for a committee meeting for the Conservative Party and chairs and a table were placed there. When Mr Elsegood's father came home from work, he was furious about this, as he was a staunch Labour man himself and so he threw all the chairs outside on the pavement and pasted large Labour posters over the Conservative ones. After that episode, it was decided that the Elsegood family would move to other accommodation.[6]

Mr Hardcastle's Memories

David Hardcastle was born in Markham Street, Haxby Road in 1933. Much of the housing in the area was built at the end of the 19th century in the form of solid terraces. The better examples had a small garden at the front, but other streets had houses which opened directly on to the pavement. His house had a front room with a bay window, a living room, a kitchen and scullery on the ground floor. There was a small back yard with a coal house, a shed and an outside toilet which often froze in the very cold winters, which were common when he was a lad. The bedrooms had open fireplaces, but fires were only lit in them when a family member was very sick. He recalled the large number of corner shops in the area which made it rarely necessary to go into town for day to day shopping. Within a small radius of his street could be found Brydon's butcher's, a post office, a baker's a milkman's yard, a greengrocer, several general stores, an off-licence and three fish and chip shops. On Haxby Road itself there was a newsagents, a butcher, two more bakers, a corsetiere and Duckworth's cycle shop. One shop which Mr Hardcastle remembered well was the Co-op in Lowther Street which disappeared in the sixties. This shop was the largest retailer in the area. At the Clarence Street end of Penley's Grove street stood branches of two well known firms, Hutchinson's grocer and Crow's pork butchers.[7]

Mrs Fairclough's Memories

Mrs Cynthia Fairclough, née Collins, lived in Hill's Court in the 1930's. This was a square of five small cottage-type houses, now demolished, which stood next to St. Maurice's Church, on Lord Mayor's Walk. Her father drove a van for Barton's confectioners, which delivered bread and cakes into rural areas. Her mother worked at Blackstones, a second hand clothes shop, which was once next to Bell's fish shop, on Lord Mayors Walk. This clothes shop received boxes of second hand clothes from gentry and well to do families around York. The boxes would cost about a £1. Mrs Fairclough's mother only received a small wage but was allowed the pick of the clothes in the boxes. Her mother's parents, Mr and Mrs Brodie had the lease of the Unicorn public house in Lord Mayor's Walk, in the 1920's. This pub was demolished in the 1960's when the road was widened and the space it once occupied is now Monk Garage.

Mrs Fairclough recalled a sad incident that happened in her family in the 1940's. Her granddad, Mr Brodie, worked part-time at St. Georges cinema in Castlegate. He was set on by two gypsy lads, whom he had caught stealing light bulbs from the cinema. In the attack, Mr Brodie fell to the ground and hit his head on the concrete pavement, he later died from his injuries. A verdict of manslaughter was retuned on his attackers.

In the early 1950's, Mrs Fairclough opened a hairdresser's shop at 60 Penley's

Cross Keys Public House, Penley's Grove Street. Demolished 1960's.
(Courtesy of Y.C.A.)

Grove Street, known as "Cynthia's". This was just opposite the Cross Keys public house. She recalled that this pub was quite small but had a side entrance to an out-sales. This contained a plank-like seat on which customers sat and chattered and often drank their purchases. She also remembered some of her customers that frequented her shop. There was Mrs Annie Lyth, who let rooms in her house at Penley's Grove Street to theatrical people. Phyllis Calvert was a regular visitor. Mrs Lyth was a larger than life character, Mrs Fairclough recalled, very sociable, and very hard working. She also remembered the Lake, Lovely, Wheatley, Limbert, Sadds, Rymers and Brown families. Her shop, along with many others in her street, was closed in the clearance schemes of the 1960's.[8]

Mrs Betty Bamford, née Nutt, who lived in Penley's Grove Street for many years, remembered the Sadd family that owned the fruit warehouse. Mr Frederick Sadd had opened a greengrocers shop in Goodramgate in the 1930s. This shop was always known as the "banana shop" as its windows were full of bananas, although other fruit were available. The green bananas were stored in a warehouse at the beginning of Penley's Grove Street. In the 1950's Mr George Sadd, the founder's son, closed the Goodramgate shop and formed the business into a limited company to concentrate exclusively in wholesale fruit and vegetables. The warehouse in Penley's Grove Street was extended, a joiners shop and two adjoining houses were acquired and it was all turned into a garage for the companies fleet of eight vehicles. These were used to distribute produce daily from the docks at Hull and Liverpool to local retailers.

Mrs Bamford also recalled that Rymer's undertakers had moved into No. 17, Penley's Grove Street in 1958. This firm had been founded by Mr James Rymer, at premises in St. Andrewgate in 1848. In 1967, the adjoining property in Penley's Grove Street, No. 15, was acquired and the business transferred there. Rymer's undertakers are still operating from these premises today, managed by the founders great grandson Mr David Rymer.[9]

Mr Woodcock's Memories

Mr Dennis Woodcock lived in Emerald Street when he was young and attended Park Grove School. He recalled some of the teacher in the 1940's. There was Mr Wadham the science master, and Bert Whincup who took them for wood work. He always kept a bottle of beer in his drawer to drink when thirsty and would hit you with anything that came to hand. Mr Faucett had a short cane he used for hitting your finger tips, if caught chattering to much. Mr Woodcock also recalled the head teacher Mr Jones, who died suddenly just before the end of the War, and that the new Head was a Mr Wilson. During the War years Mr Woodcock was head prefect and also won the York School Swimming Championship in 1950. When he was older he joined Park Grove Youth Club and recalled playing handball in the hall with an upturned bench for a goal. At weekends he helped out at Mr Ashcroft's boot and shoe shop which was in

Emerald street. His job was to rip out the old soles from shoes sent to be soled and heeled. He also remembered a Mrs Salmon, who owned a monkey that she kept in a cage in her front room. During the summer months Mr Woodcock would play football in the street with his friends and recalled a man, who could only walk with crutches, always joined in.[10]

Mrs Sheila Littlefair, who was a Bonney before she was married, also lived in the Groves when she was a girl. She went to St. Thomas' Church School and remembered the Headmaster, a Mr Futer. He was only a small man, she recalled and lived in a house on Wigginton Road. She remembered as she went to school passing the blacksmith's forge in the yard next to the Castle Howard Ox public house. This pub was always known as "Bill's pub" as the Landlord was "Big Bill" Fairless, one of the area's characters.[11]

Mr Pickard's Memories

Mr Pickard took over the newsagent's and post office at the corner of Monkgate and Penley's Grove Street, now Plaskitt & Plaskitt, in the 1970's. Previous owners of this shop had been Mr Scrimshire and then Mr Walker. Mr Pickard recalled some of the shops in Monkgate in the 1950's and 60's. He remembered the garage near Monk Bar was owned by Hill and Mercer, and Mr Harold Smith had a garage next to St. Maurices Church. There was a garage near Monk Bridge roundabout but it is now houses. Sid Haw had his garage on the corner of Lowther Street and Huntington Road. Mrs Baram owned a second hand clothes shop near St. Wilfrid's School and Bowman's Removals had furniture depositories on both sides of Monkgate. In 1959 the buildings near the County Hospital, belonging to this firm collapsed, trapping one man inside. Fortunately they were able to rescue him. Mr Pickard remembered that Mr Brook had his fish shop under Monk Bar for a long time and Cox the shoe repairers were the other side of the Bar. He recalled Binns who sold tyres and the Monkgate and Jersey Dairy Company at the corner of Agar Street. A shop that sold beds took over from them. Bob Trotter had his cycle shop near the hospital and Mr Moyser the plumber was at No. 28 Monkgate. Mr Pickard's brother had a fish shop in Walpole Street since the 1940's.[12]

Mr Pickard recalled the Lund family, that lived in Monkgate. This family had owned a grocery shop in Goodramgate. This shop, which was one of the last privately owned family concerns in York, was opened by Alfred Lund in the early years of the last century. Mr Henry Lund, who lived at No. 68 Monkgate was the last head of the firm, retiring in 1965. He was well known in York and described as an outspoken Yorkshire man, with a great interest in cricket. His brother, Richard, who had lived at No. 73 Monkgate, also a keen sportsman, ran the Huntington branch.[13]

Haw's Garage, corner of Lowther Street and Huntington Road. c.1950.
(Courtesy of Y.R.L.)

Mrs Cole's Memories

Mrs Maureen Cole, nee Wheatley, grew up in the Groves also. Her Grandfather Mr Jack Sinton, had lived at No. 13 Townend Street, which was quite a big house compared to many in the area. Mrs Cole lived at 24 Townend Street when she was young. This house was only a "two up and two down" with a scullery with a stone sink, cold tap and a copper in the corner. Outside in the yard there was an outside toilet and a tin bath for bath night in front of the fire. She remembered some of her neighbours from her youth. Next door there was the Questa family, they were Italians, a lovely family she recalled. They had only one son Albert who never married. Mr Holmes, who was a big man and "Big" Bill Fairless who was so huge he filled the door of the Castle Howard Ox and could drink a gill of beer. In the summer months people would often sit outside their front doors and talk to neighbours. One lady, she recalled would often sit outside, peeling shallots. There were often a few disturbances when the pubs closed. Once there was a man playing his bagpipes late at night, which didn't go down very well with the residents.

Mrs Cole, or Maureen Wheatley as she was then, was married from 24 Townend Street to Mr Peter Cole, who was the local policeman. Mr Cole was in the police force for thirty years and although he was on the beat for many years, eventually became a Detective Sergeant working for the C.I.D. He was respected in the area and well known to the local residents and could go round to see the parents of lads, who may have been misbehaving, knowing that they would believe what he said and be strict with their children.

Mrs Cole who still lives in the Groves, thought that the demolitions of the 1960's changed the character of the area. When she was young people were always willing to help one another and there seemed to be a stronger community spirit.

Clarence Club Walking Match. Wheatley family on left. c.1950.
(Courtesy of Mrs M Cole)

Many former residents, re-housed or moved away from the area remember their days there with nostalgia and affection. People didn't have as many possessions in their homes as now and were not so afraid of break-ins and burglaries. One old lady recalled that her neighbours often remarked that if anyone wanted to pinch anything from their house, they would have to take something in first. This she believed was very true in many cases and led to a happier lifestyle.[14]

Chapter VIII. Notes and References.
1. Information supplied by Mr R. Lake, Towthorpe Road.
2. Information supplied by Mrs D Ros, Huntington Road.
3. Information supplied by Mr F Myers, 1 Park Crescent.
4. Information supplied by Mr And Mrs N Marshall, Stockton on the Forest.
5. Information supplied by Mr Mr A Martindale, Heworth Hall Drive.
6. Information supplied by Mr B Elsegood, Moatfield, Osbaldwick.
7. Information supplied by Mr D Hardcastle, late Peel Close, Heslington.
8. Information supplied by Mrs C Fairclough, Whitby Drive.
9. Information supplied by Mrs B Bamford. Y.E.P. 25.9.1967. Y.E.P. -
10. Information supplied by Mr D Woodcock, Meadowfield Way.
11. Information supplied by Mrs S Littlefair, née Bonney, Priory Street.
12. Information supplied by Mr H Pickard, Acomb.
13. Information supplied by Mrs M Dent, late Grovesnor Terrace.
14. Information supplied by Mrs M Cole, Townend Street.

Houses in Pilgrim Street. Ready for demolition. c.1960. *(courtesy of Y.C.A.)*

Demolition and After

In 1957, plans were submitted and passed by York Council for the compulsory purchase of most of the small houses in the Groves area. The houses on the outer edges of this area were demolished first, such as Cole Street, Brook Street and Pilgrim Street. These contained some of the oldest houses in the area, some had been built as early as 1830. Then, most of the houses in Jackson Street, Townend Street, March Street and Garden Street were demolished. The larger houses at the beginning of Penley's Grove Street were left but the smaller houses in the central area were pulled down. A few houses at the start of Lowther Street remained but most of that street, apart from the building that had been St. Hilda's Home, was demolished. The small streets that stood in front of Park Grove School, such as Bedford Street, Princess Street and Duke Street were also earmarked for demolition at this time. The area where Newbiggin Street, Bearpark Square and Groves Place had stood became a large car park for the City. Many of the owners of condemned properties felt that they were poorly compensated for their homes.[1]

Garden Street, showing Millard's Newsagent's. c.1960. *(Courtesy of Y.C.A.)*

Many of the residents were reluctant to move especially the older people and some were so stressed about it all that they became ill. They felt isolated from their families and the close community they had always known. When the large blocks of flats and maisonettes were built in Lowther Street, Penley's Grove Street and Townend Street, where the old houses had stood, many former residents moved back into these. However they found a different area than the one they had left. Most of the smaller public houses, such as Cross Keys, the Bowling Green and the Dove in Jackson Street were demolished. The Magpie and Reindeer were knocked down, but rebuilt on the same sites in a more modern design. The Punch Bowl and the Castle Howard Ox, two Victorian pubs, were left standing. The Bowling Green Pub was bought from the brewery in 1966. Plans were passed then for twelve one bedroom flats and six garages. Dent's Joinery Works moved to a site in Layerthorpe at this time also.[2]

St. Hilda's Home closed in the early 1950s and the children were moved to Clifton. The building was then used for an occupation centre for Mental Welfare. The York Boys' Club took it over as their headquarters in the 1970's, when the one in Layerthorpe closed. It is now a centre for One Parent families and a youth club. Most of the shops were moved to Lowther Street opposite St. Thomas's Church.[3] The school next to this church was closed in 1957 but was used by St. John's College until the 1990's. It was eventually demolished in 1995 and a new building built to accommodate offices for the Probation Services. In the 1990's £1,150 was raised to restore two windows in St. Thomas' Church. A memorial window was installed, dedicated to the memory of Alison Fearnley, who tragically died from cancer aged only 19 years.[4]

The Grey Coat School closed in the 1960's and was used as the School Clinic, later to become a Health Centre. St. Wilfrid's School underwent a total refurbishment in the 1990s. The boys' senior school of Park Grove School closed

St. Maurice's Church. Demolished 1967.

in 1980 and this school became a junior school. In 1997 a fire destroyed most of this building but it was rebuilt and opened again the following year. Archbishop Holgate's School on Lord Mayor's Walk moved to Hull Road in 1961, and the nearby St. John's Senior School closed in 1965. In the 1970's St. John's College amalgamated with the training college at Ripon and became Ripon St. John. At the start of the 21st century plans have been made to reunite both halves of the College and bring it all to York, where it will be called York St. John, but under the jurisdiction of Leeds University.[5]

The lofty edifice, St. Maurice's Church that had stood on the corner of Monkgate and Lord Mayor's Walk, was demolished in 1967 as part of the inner ring road scheme. Now only a few grave stones set in a grassy area tell of its existence. A new building to house the D.S.S. was built in the 1970's, next to the site of this Church, were once Smith's garage and Baram's shop had stood. The small houses that had comprised Hill's Court and Wheatley's buildings, that were situated next to the church at the beginning of Lords Mayor's Walk, had been taken down in the 1930's. The Unicorn public house, on the opposite side of the road was demolished in the late 1950's to widen the road. The Baron family were the last landlords. Monk Garage now stands in its place. The Bay Horse public house changed its name to Keystones in the 1990's. The Atha family were the licensees of this pub for many years.[6]

Bulmer's selling services and fishing tackle dealers took over the premises that had once been Wrightson's, later Metcalfe's, fruit shop, on the corner of Monkgate and Lord Mayor's Walk. At the opposite side of Monkgate at the corner of St. Maurice's Road, Hutchinson's store and post office were removed

Unicorn public house, on Lord Mayor's Walk. Demolished late 1950's.
(Courtesy of Y.E.P.)

to widen this corner. Haigh's butcher's shop remained on the other corner of St. Maurice's Road until the 1980s, when with other buildings on this corner, were converted to a hotel, Monkgate Cloisters. St. Maurice's Church Hall was taken over by the hospital as a remedial gym in the 1960s. The small courts and streets that had been in this area such as Plane Tree and Barker Hill, had been demolished in the 1930s. Houses in Jewbury and Orchard Street that were at the Layerthorpe end of St. Maurice's Road were taken down in the 1960s. Sainsbury's built their store and car park in this area and on land that had once been a Jewish cemetery. Sainsbury's Stores extended to land near Monk Bridge over the old Gas Works site.[7] The County Hospital closed in 1977 and was used as offices for the Yorkshire Water Board for many years. In the 1990's a private consortium converted the old hospital buildings into luxury flats. Many of the large houses in Monkgate were converted into flats or residences for doctors in the 1960's. No. 38, the Rev. Wellbeloved's old house, later used by St. Maurices Church as a Rectory, was taken over by the Knights of St. Columba, a Roman Catholic club. Garbutt and Elliott, charted accountants moved into George Hudson's house, in the 1970's. A malt kiln, later used as a store, which had stood behind this house was demolished in the 1990's to make room for a car park.[8]

Haw's garage, which had stood at the end of Lowther Street fronting Huntington Road from the 1920's, has just recently been demolished to make way for a modern housing development. This garage, founded by Sydney William Haw, opened in 1929 and was part of the old community. In the 1990s, although run then by a board of directors, boasted a work force of more than thirty.[9] Sadd's old fruit warehouse in Penley's Grove Street, where many bananas were stored in the 1940s and 50s has just recently closed also. The Anne Harrison Hospital and old chapel were demolished in the 1960's but new modern alms houses and a residential home were built in the same street, near the original site. The York Union Workhouse on Huntington Road became The Grange and later St. Mary's Hospital for geriatric patients. In the 1990's new modern housing was erected in the grounds of the old Workhouse building.[10]

Most people that have been re-housed or moved away from the Groves and Monkgate have happy memories of their days there. They thought that the demolition of the streets that stood in the middle areas of the Groves signalled the end of an era. Many felt that the heart of this area had been torn out. They remembered the close community spirit that once existed here. Three or more generations of the same family lived near each other. Doors could be left open without fear of burglary and people helped one another especially those that had fallen on hard times. Now most of the people with families have gone. The older people feel isolated in their flats. Only a few shops remain in this area, grouped together at the end of Lowther Street. Many of the larger houses have been turned into flats for young single people. There has been trouble with drugs and crime in certain areas.

No longer do people sit outside their little houses in the Groves, the men smoking their pipes, the women knitting and chatting. No longer do groups of children play in the streets, girls skipping under a long washing line, boys playing endless games of football and cricket. Nowadays, there is only a constant stream of traffic travelling along Penley's Grove Street and Lowther Street in the one way system that now exists. Perhaps the sound of children's voices in the playground of Park Grove School is a poignant reminder of that community, that lived and worked, married and brought up their families in those small houses in the streets and courts that was Monkgate and The Groves.

Pickard's newsagent's, corner of Monkgate and Penley's Grove Street. c.1970.
(Courtesy of Mr H Pickard)

Demolition and After. Notes and References
 1. Y.C.A. Compulsory Purchase Orders (C.P.O. 1959).
 2. Y.E.P. 1957. 1959-66.
 3. Kelly's Directories (1950-70).
 4. Y.E.P. August 1957.
 5. Y.E.P. 1990.
 6. Information supplied by Mr M Mead, Fulford.
 7. Y.C.A. C.P.O. 1930. 1950's 1960's.
 8. Information supplied by Mr and Mrs M Powell, 74 Monkgate.
 9. Y.R.L. Newspaper Index.
 10. Kelly's 1960's.

Park Grove Football Team. c.1954. Cup winners 1954-55.
Pete Mowbray (Teacher), D Powell, R Goodhall, H Jones, D Sturdy, D Goslep, R Hodson, N Goodway, D Boyes, E Spaven, D Armgill, D Walker. *(Courtesy of Mr D Sturdy)*

Park Grove School Form 3A. 1947.

Back Row (left): Maurice Clinton, Ken Beevers, Geo Wells, David Barton, Brian Pottage, John Robinson, John Ward, George, Gordon Roberts.
Second Row: Brian Smith, Colin Watson, Ray Bowman, Tommy Bucknall, - , Pauline Broadhead, Yvonne Wheatley, Edna Watson, Jackie Burbridge, Doreen Powell, Norman Fairclough, Brian Darley, B. Bains, Denis Woodcock.
Third Row: Sheila Gilbank, Rebecca Todd, - , Marjorie Bramley, Irene Speck, - , Joan Quin, Agnes Narsmith, Audrey Brough, Joan Baird.
Front Row: Oliver, Ken Beaton, - , Eddie Watson, David Brewer, John Morton, John Borwell.   *(Courtesy of Mr D. Woodcock)*

Park Crescent Coronation Party 1953. (*Courtesy of Mr F Myers*)

Monkgate. Late 1960's.

LOWTHER STREET.
7 Huntington road to 86 Haxby road.
Left side.
1 Boyes Wm
3 Dixon Norman
9 Treloar Percy
11 Boggett Wm. H. N
13 Boultwood Jn. A
15 Holmes Jsph
17 Hillyer Geo
19 Baxter Mrs. Mary J
21 Richmond Maurice T
23 Taylor Leslie
25 Gill Hy
...here is Bowling Green ln
27 Nicholson Chas. S
29 Cartwright Eric
31 Buck Jim
33 Mayfield Harold J
35 Robinson Roy
37 Ferguson —
39 Wood Rd
39 Morhamer Mrs. Dorothy
41 Ellis Mark
45 Bushby Fred M
47 Hansell Thos
49 Kemp-Webster Wm. C
51/53 Benson's for Bikes
55 Benson Jas
57 Phillips Chas. Irwin, hairdresser
59 Flatley Mrs. Lily M. beer retlr
61 Pointing Thos. fruitr
63 Hewson Arth
65 Passmore Jn. W. genl. dlr
.........here is Jackson st.........
67 Smith Geo H
69 Elsworth Jn
71 Ashworth Fras. A
York Co-operative Society Ltd. butchers
York Co-operative Society Ltd. grocers
..........here is March st..........
77 Ward Mark
79 Ayres Mrs. Ethel
81 Smallwood Wm
83 Raftery Mrs. Annie
85 Taylor Hy. J
87 Cairns Jn. J
89 Bufton Ronald H
91 Beautiman G. Ralph
93 Peacock Cyril
95 Rogers Norman W
97 Bootland Arth
99 Hardwick Leonard
101 Holmes Dennis R
..........here is Eldon st..........
103 Watson Thos. W. fried fish dlr
105 Nicholson Mrs. Eliz
107 Hogan Rd
109 Broadhead Mrs. Edith E
111 Vince Fredk. J
113 Jarvis Peter
115 Johnson Mrs
117 Clark Edwd
119 Waugh Rt
121 Fisher Hy. G. A
123 Walder Wm
125 Martin Ronald H
127 Pearson Mrs. Rachel
129 Lee Mrs. Amelia
131 Sewter Geo. W
133 Douglas Wm. A. N
137 Brotherton Leslie
139 Barker Miss M
141 Lewis Edwd. S
143 Paylor Anthony G
145 Crosby Mrs
147 Edson Ernest A
149 Mills Mrs.Margt. shopkp
.. here is Little Silver st
151 Fieldhouse Gregory
153 Bryan Ronald
155 McClusky Wm. H
159 Parker Geo. R
161 Plows Albt. E
167 McKevitt Arth

Right side
Haw's Garage
.... here is Park ter ....
26 Dyson Mrs
28 Hardcastle Jn. R
30 Toyne Geo. H
32 Hopwood Leonard W
...... here is Bedford st ....
34 Arkless J. R. bldr
36 Bradley Kenneth
38 Thom David
.... here is Duke st ....
42 Culken Bernard
44 Snowball Jn. D
44 Garrett Oswald Geo. tur commssn. agt
46 Krawiec Michl
48 Bramhall Wltr
50 Lee Kenneth
52 Gawthrop Harry
54 Lewis Maelgwyn J
56 McCreary —
58 Thompson Sidney N
...... here is Princess st .....
60 Stoakes Keir
62 Gibson Mrs. Annie E
64 Hall Noel
66 Newby Frank
68 Hall Jn
72 Tupman Edwd
74 Hebditch Bert
76 Pickering Miss A
78 Plummer Mrs. Eliz. M
...... here is Brownlow st ......
80 Rennie Jas
82 Scaife Wm
84 Gorman Jas. A
84 Mental Welfare Dept. Occupation Centre
86 Oliver Wm
88a. Brook Jn
90 Page Mrs. Frances A. shopkpr
.... here is Eldon st ....
92 Harrison Mrs. Emma J
94 Allan Mrs. Annie
96 Dossor Hy
98 Burnett Jn. L
100 Dodd Mrs. Ella May

Kelly's Extract. Lowther Street (1957)

PENLEY'S GROVE STREET.
61 Monkgate to 1 Townend st.
Right side.
1 York Tyre Service
Sadd F. A. & Son Ltd. who, fruit mers
3 Allen Maurice
5 Reeder Mrs. Lily M
7 Evans Mrs. G
Oulds F. V. & Co. plumber
Groves Working Men' Club
.... here is Groves la ....
9 Lyth Geo
11 Gledhill Geo. E
13 Rooke Eric
15 Brown Eric
17 Ebelthite Jn. D
19 Jackson Eric D
21 Steel Thos
23 Weir Jas
25 Miller Mrs. S. A
27 Jost Jsph. M
29 Leach Miss Helen
31 Gill Chas. W
33 Hinde Rt. L
35 Ashton Mrs. Minnie
37 Skilbeck Laurence
37 Shepherd Miss Joan, ladies' hairdrssr
39 Raby Wltr
41 Nutt Wltr
43 Bruce Andrew S
43 Crowe Rt. & Sons Ltd. who. grocers
45 Thompson Mrs. Ellen, animal food dlr
49 Cuthbert Jas. C
49a, Brown Chas. H
49b. Wilson Wilfred M
51 Knaggs Harold
53 Wray Laurence
55 Mills Harold
57 Kerrigan Chas
59 Lawson Jn. G
59 Lovely's Fisheries
.... here is March st ....
61 Cunningham Dennis, toy dlr
61 Parker Alfd
63 Lee A. grocer
67 Moore Wm
69 Hall Fredk
71 Payne Geo. H
73 Kelsey Stanley C
75 Cross Keys Inn
79 Bevan Jn. R
81 Hilton Albt. G
81a, Simmons Rt. A. shopkpr
83 Hibbett Stanley

Left side.
2 Ebor Mudguards, motor accessories dlrs
2 Mortimer Rt
4 Leeming Mrs. Anne
6 Schofield Wm. H
8 Wetherill Mrs. E. M
10 Steele Mrs. Gertrude
16 Slater Mrs. Margt
.... here is Groves la ....
18 Graysmark Mrs. Mabel, grocer
18 Graysmark Arth. Edwd
20 Rhodes Thos
22 Sheppard Wm. A
24 Hutson Mrs. Ada
26 Holmes Miss Edith
28 Hunt Mrs. Mary
30 Jackson Mrs. Alice M
32 Rickell Mrs
34 Thompson Mrs. M
36 Abbott Norman
.... here is St. John's cres ...

Harrison's Hospital.
1 Lightfoot Miss Violet
2 Cooper Mrs. S. E
3 Jackson Miss A
4 Byworth Mrs
5 Booth Mrs. M
6 Brown Mrs
7 Lingwood Mrs. Emma
8 Swann Mrs. Laura

46 Quill Geo
48 Upton Mrs. Violet A
50 Patterson Peter N
52 Usher Philip
52 Usher Fred
54 Ridsdale Alfd. H. butcher
.... here is Abbot st ....
56 Reindeer Inn
58 Vacher Saml
60 Bramhill Hy
60 Cynthia, ladies' hairdrssr
62 Wells Mrs. Ethel
64 Smithers Mrs. Doris
66 Young Wm
68 Kidd Jas
70 Gladdish Fred
70 Merrett Arth. E
.... here is Eldon st ....
72 Elliotts (Yorks) Ltd. grocers
72 Pratt Harold
74 Fletcher Mrs. Gertrude
76 Markham Miss Alice
78 Lupton J

YORK 6†

Kelly's Extract. Penley's Grove Street (1959)

152 MON   YORK

MONK AVENUE.
1 Stockton lane.
(No thoroughfare.)
15 Rankin Donald M
16 Burrow Arth. G
17 North Miss
18 Nicholson Mrs. G
20 Barnett Harry G
21 Linfoot Cyril
24 Coates Ted
25 Hinchcliffe Hy

MONK BAR CHMBRS.
See Monkgate.

MONK BAR COURT.
2 Goodramgate.
(No thoroughfare.)
3 Myton Cyril
4 Littlewood Mrs
5 Oundall Mrs. Mary E
6 Croft Miss Dorothy
7 Ryder Mrs. Jane A

MONK BRIDGE.
Over River Foss, joining Monkgate & Heworth.

MONKGATE.
Monk bar to Monk bridge.
Left side.
1 Chalk D. V. radio dlr
3 Hudson Jas. W. butcher
... here is Bowman's yard ...
  Hill & Mercer, motor engnrs. (Monk Bar garage)
  Sewing Machine Service (L. Weeks)
5 Wrightson David & Geo. fruitrs
...here is Lord Mayor's walk...
  St. Maurice's Church
  Smith H. D. motor car garage (The Garage)
11 Clarkson H. & Son, genl. engnrs. (Monk Bar works)
17 Baram A. M. & F. B. wardrobe dlrs
17 Baram Frank B
19/21 St. Wilfrid's Convent
19/21 St. Wilfrid's R.C. Primary School
19/21 St. Wilfrid's Secondary Modern School
29 Black Horse Inn
29a, Major & Co. Ltd. petroleum company
  Grey Coat School (girls)
37 Bowman Jas. & Sons, furniture depository
39 (bottom flat) Cooker Miss Helen E

39 (flat a) Smith David
39 (flat b) Davis Mrs. L
  Monkgate Methodist Chrch
45 Waller Jn
45 Sadler Claud
45 Potter Fredk
49 (flat 1) Dykes Mrs. M
49 Woodthorpe Geoffrey
49 Ellis Rt
51 Metcalfe Mrs. Emily
53 Haxby Miss Bella
55 Larman Geo. E
57 Nottingham Mrs. R. draper
57 Nottingham Clyde A
59 Scrimshire P. & A. E. confectioners
... here is Penley's Grove st ...
61 Grosvenor Guest House
61 Cobb Frank S
65 Buttery G. E. & Sons, joiners
65 Dixon Miss Evelyn
67 Scrimshaw Anthony O
69 Buckley-Marshall Miss L
71 Whiteley Harold
73 Lund Rd
75 Craven Frank
  Haw's Garage Petrol & Service Station
77 Savage Jn. A
79 Foster Albt. J

Right side
2 Brook G. E. & Sons, fishmongers
4 Bay Horse P.H
6 Hutchinson Bros. grocers, & post office
6a, Fortescue Stuart N
... here is St. Maurice rd ...
8 Haigh Jn. R. butcher

Monk Bar Chambers.
Dossor Jn. M.I.C.E. consulting engnr
10 Martin —
12 Johnson Wm
14 Meadowcroft J. W. boot repr
16 Abbott F. saw repr
18 Trotter R. G. cycle repr
20/26 Bowman Jas. & Sons, furniture depositories
26 Dossor Jn. M.I.C.E. consulting engnr
28 Moyser Thos. & Son, plumbers
28 Moyser Herbt. E
  County Hospital (York (A) & Tadcaster Hospital Management Committee)
36 Jones Katharine Rounsfell M.B., Ch.B., D.P.H. physcn
36 d'Andria Miss Vivienne M.B., Ch.B., L.R.C.S., M.R.C.P. physcn. & surgn
36 Gray Miss Mary E. S., M.B., B.S. physcn. & surgn

38 Bulmer Rev. Edwd. Stanley North M.A. (rector of St. Maurice's)
38 Society for the Propagation of the Gospel
38 St. Maurice's Boys' Preparatory School
40 Clark Arth
40a, Northern Distributors Ltd. motor fctrs
42 Binns Rt. B. & Son, motor tyre fctrs
44 Smith-Shand Mrs. V. M
46 Ruralime Supplies Co. lime mers
46 Ridings Construction Co. Ltd. building contrctrs
48 Kleen-e-ze Brush Co. Ltd
48a, Spratt R. grocer
48/52 Monkgate & Jersey Dairy Co. Ltd. dairymen
.... here is Agar st ....
62 Hatton Jn. C
62 Ensor Anthony
64 Everard Colin
64 Senescall Jn
64 Preece Rt. G
66 Goodson Peter H
66 Warrener Miss E
66 Cretney Philip
66 Clancy Miss
66 Chapman Thos
68 Lund Hy
70 Jackson Arth
72 Willans Mrs. C. B
74 Walker Jas. H
76 Wickins Mrs. Anne
78 Cooke Percy
80 Coleman Wm. D
82 Lack Albt. J
.... here is Foss Bank ....
Monk Bridge Construction Co. Ltd. structural engnrs

MONKTON ROAD.
77 Byland avenue.
(No thoroughfare.)
Left side.
1 Holliday Wilfred
3 Parker Victor
5 Gamble Leonard
7 England Mrs. S
9 Airey Paul B
11 Taylor Jsph. W
13 O'Brien Kenneth R
15 Elliott Leslie R
17 O'Neill Jn
19 Aldersey Albt
21 Watkinson Fredk
23 Carlton Alwyn M
25 Sawyer Arth
27 Ellis Mrs. E
29 Brown Arth
31 Guller Wm
33 Hick Mrs. I
35 Wilstrop Lawrence A
37 Darnbrough Eric
39 Young Harry P

Kelly's Extract. Monkgate (1957)